Navigating the Free Trade–Fair Trade Fault-Lines

Michael J. Trebilcock

Faculty Emeritus and formerly Chair in Law and Economics, Faculty of Law, University of Toronto, Canada

 Edward Elgar
PUBLISHING

Cheltenham, UK • Northampton, MA, USA

Published by
Edward Elgar Publishing Limited
The Lypiatts
15 Lansdown Road
Cheltenham
Glos GL50 2JA
UK

Edward Elgar Publishing, Inc.
William Pratt House
9 Dewey Court
Northampton
Massachusetts 01060
USA

Paperback edition 2021

A catalogue record for this book
is available from the British Library

Library of Congress Control Number: 2020952709

This book is available electronically in the **Elgar**online
Law subject collection
http://dx.doi.org/10.4337/9781800882362

ISBN 978 1 80088 235 5 (cased)
ISBN 978 1 80088 236 2 (eBook)
ISBN 978 1 80220 511 4 (paperback)

Printed and bound in Great Britain by TJ Books Limited, Padstow, Cornwall

Contents

Preface

I have been teaching international trade law for about 35 years at the University of Toronto Law School to very talented law students who all have prior degrees in a wide range of disciplines, and also to a sprinkling of graduate students from law, economics, political science, public policy, and global affairs from around the world. Over this period, I have also taught international trade law or a related course on law and development as a Visiting Professor at NYU School of Law, University of Pennsylvania Law School, University of Virginia School of Law, Yale Law School, Harvard Law School, Johns Hopkins University, Tsinghua Law School in Beijing, the University of Hong Kong Faculty of Law, and the National University of Singapore Faculty of Law. From the various interactions and engagements with students in these various parts of the world, certain key questions about international trade law and policy seem regularly to perplex or provoke them. It is these questions that motivate this short introduction to these issues, which I hope will be of value and interest to the general and time-constrained reader. Readers who wish to pursue some of these issues further might usefully refer to the book by myself and Joel Trachtman, *Advanced Introduction to International Trade Law* (2nd edn, Edward Elgar Publishing, 2020).

Acknowledgements

I am indebted for helpful comments on earlier drafts of this book to Ben Alarie, David Beatty, Kevin Davis, Tony Duggan, Andrew Green, Ed Iacobucci, Rozemin Keshvani, Anthony Niblett, and Joel Trachtman, and to Alissa Wang for exceptional research assistance.

I. The free trade–fair trade fault-lines in historical context

A) THE CONTEMPORARY CONTEXT

The formation of the General Agreement on Tariffs and Trade (the GATT) in 1947, initially with 23 member countries, was part of a trilogy of new international economic institutions flowing out of the Bretton Woods Agreement of 1944 between Britain and the US. The International Monetary Fund was charged with stabilizing international exchange rates while the World Bank was charged with providing financial assistance to developing countries. The GATT's mandate was progressive multilateral trade liberalization. For most of the following post-war decades, international trade policy was a low-visibility, low-politics affair, focused on periodic negotiating rounds designed primarily to reduce tariffs reciprocally on cross-border trade in goods. However, the Uruguay Round negotiating agenda from 1986 to 1993 extended well beyond reciprocal tariff reductions to a wide range of non-tariff barriers to trade, including: intellectual property rights; agricultural subsidies; food and product standards; government procurement; the regulation of foreign direct investment; trade in services; and subsidies more generally.

This multi-decade period of relative tranquility in international trade relations was shattered most dramatically, if symbolically, on November 30, 1999, when a Ministerial meeting of members of the World Trade Organization (the successor to the GATT as of 1995 and now with more than 160 members) had been convened for Seattle, ostensibly to plan the agenda for a new negotiating round. Delegates to the meeting were met with an estimated 50,000 protesters who blocked hotel and conference entrances and exits by way of advancing a number of critiques of WTO agreements and policies, not always consistent with one another: trade union representatives in the US protesting job losses in the US manufacturing sector to low wage developing countries; environmental groups protesting WTO dispute settlement decisions that seemed to preclude trade restrictions designed to protect endangered species, such as dolphin and turtles in foreign waters; labour activists protesting exploitative labour conditions in many developing countries, including child labour and bonded labour and international NGOs protesting the lack of access by many developing countries to developed countries' markets for agricultural products. Dispersed amongst these mostly peaceful protesters were assorted anarchists who broke store windows and looted contents and damaged police cars, leading the mayor of Seattle to declare a state of emergency and WTO Ministerial delegates to abandon the meeting, and adjourn it to the relatively safe haven of Doha in Qatar two years later.

Despite the dramatic coverage of the Battle in Seattle in media around the world, the warning signs of discontent with the international economic system had already been evident for some time. These included actions around the vigorously contested Canadian federal election of 1988 over the ratification of the Canada–US Free Trade Agreement; the equally strenuously contested US Presidential elections in 1992 over the extension of this Agreement to include Mexico in a North American Free Trade Agreement; the Mexican peso crisis in 1994; the Asian financial crisis in 1997; and the AIDS crisis in the 1990s, provoking criticisms that the Trade-related Intellectual Property Agreement (TRIPS) negotiated as part of the Uruguay Round package of agreements had severely constrained the ability of poor developing countries to provide access to patented essential medicines in dealing with AIDS and other tropical diseases.

The perturbations over international trade policy so dramatically exemplified by the Battle of Seattle did not, of course, end there. The protests in Seattle were quickly followed by the Argentinian financial crisis of 2001–2002 and, of course, the global financial crisis of 2008; the Syrian refugee crisis that led to a massive influx of immigrants into the European Union in 2015; the vote in a British referendum of 2016 to leave the European Union (confirmed by a Parliamentary vote in late 2019); the US–China trade conflict initiated by the Trump Administration in 2016; and now of course the grave international health and economic implications of the calamitous coronavirus pandemic.

B) CONCEPTIONS OF FREE AND FAIR TRADE

For purposes of the discussion that follows in this book, some clarification of my understanding of the concepts of free and fair trade is appropriate. With respect to free trade, I have in mind cross-border transactions that largely reflect what would widely be viewed as mutually advantageous domestic contracts: voluntary, in the sense that sellers and buyers are sufficiently numerous that no party possesses substantial market power (bordering on monopoly or monopsony), recognizing that this is a matter of degree; informed, in the sense that buyers are reasonably well-informed about the characteristics of alternative offerings among sellers and free of major externalities that impose significant costs on involuntary third parties. Free trade may be compromised by firms or governments adopting policies that either expand or restrict trade in ways that are at variance with these conditions.

With regard to fair trade, beyond being free, as with domestic transactions, concerns might appropriately focus on the distributional impacts of cross-border transactions: on the demand side, are less advantaged citizens major beneficiaries of cross-border trade and conversely disproportionately prejudiced by the costs of trade protectionism? Or do low-priced imports put at disproportionate risk domestic employment by less advantaged workers? In turn, do some trading regimes preclude effective participation on the supply side by citizens of poorer nations? Or does freer trade principally benefit wealthier owners of mobile capital able to exploit off-shoring or outsourcing options?

Beyond issues of distributive justice, as with domestic contracting, cross-border trade may raise legitimate concerns that some forms of trade violate fundamental notions of individual autonomy and basic human dignity, and require redress or constraints, even where cross-border markets are reasonably competitive and in some cases where cross-border competition is so intense that it places severe pressure on these values (slavery in the production of goods for export being the limiting case). In some cases, these fairness concerns may be alleviated by expanding international trade, in other cases they may justify restricting trade.[1] I will elaborate on these conceptions of free and fair trade in particular contexts in the discussion that follows.

C)   THE EVOLUTION OF TRADE PATTERNS ON THE GROUND

It may be tempting to consider conflicts and controversies over international trade policies (which in their most expansive form include cross-border movement of goods; services; capital; and people – the so-called four economic freedoms)

---

[1]   Nicholas Lamp, "How Should We Think about the Winners and Losers from Globalization? Three Narratives and Their Implications for the Redesign of International Economic Agreements" (2019) 30 *European Journal of International Law* 1359.

as relatively contemporary phenomena. However, this is not true. Looking back through history to ancient times, including the first movement of our earliest ancestors out of Africa into Eurasia 70,000 years ago, international trading relations have often raised free trade–fair trade concerns, in some cases manifested at the time, in other cases from later vantage points. The evolution of early societies from hunter-gatherer groups to settled forms of agriculture gave rise to villages and later small cities and eventually nation states, and trading across these land-based boundaries was common and often mutually beneficial. The emergence of the Silk Road provided trade linkages mostly by land across Eurasia from as early as two millennia ago (although it also in the 13th and 14th centuries facilitated the Mongol invasion of Eastern Europe and the bubonic plague or Black Death that killed up to an estimated 60 per cent of the European population or up to 50 million people).

The evolution of large square rigged sailing ships, the rudder, and the magnetic compass in the early Middle Ages opened up seaborne trade from the Middle East and Eastern Mediterranean through the Red Sea across the Indian Ocean to India and China, and eventually the Spice Islands (Indonesia) to the south. The discovery of a sea route around the Cape of Good Hope to the Indian Ocean by Vasco da Gama (on behalf of Portugal) in 1488 (loosening the lock of Arab traders on the sea route from the Red Sea to the East Indies), and then the discovery by Christopher Columbus (on behalf of Spain) searching for the Northwest Passage across the Atlantic Ocean, but instead discovering the so-called New World in North and South America in 1492, all dramatically expanded cross-border trading networks. The onset of the Industrial Revolution in the late 18th century in Europe, in particular the invention of the steam engine and modern railway systems and steam ships, greatly lowered internal and external transportation costs, while the invention of the telegraph in the late 19th century greatly reduced international communication costs. The invention of containerization in the mid-20th century further reduced transportation costs, and the ICT revolution beginning in the early 1990s has had a dramatic and continuing impact on communication costs and facilitated the formation of complex and now pervasive global supply chains.[2]

However, over much of this long reach of history, less edifying features characterized much cross-border trade. From ancient empires onwards – including the Greek and Roman empires through to the Islamic and Ottoman empires, the Mongol empire, the British Empire, and the various colonial European powers, including Spain, Portugal, Holland, and France – many of these trading networks, reflected in preferential trading regimes imposed by colonizing powers on their colonies, were the product of conquest or annexation of foreign territories and the appropriation of the land, natural resources, and often inhabitants of these territories through slavery or other forms of conscripted or indentured labour, in many cases decimating the indigenous population by force or infectious diseases. The most dramatic example of such factors at play is the Atlantic slave trade, where, over the 16th to the 18th century, 12 million slaves were shipped by slave traders from various regions of Africa (with a loss of more than a million lives in transit) to the colonies in the New World, where slave labour was an essential economic ingredient in promoting plantation economies in the Caribbean, various countries in South America, and the southern states in

---

[2]   William Bernstein, *A Splendid Exchange: How Trade Shaped the World* (New York: Atlantic Monthly Press, 2008); Richard Baldwin, *The Great Convergence: Information Technology and the New Globalization* (Cambridge, MA: Harvard University Press, 2016). Jeffrey D. Sachs, *The Ages of Globalization: Geography, Technology, and Institutions* (New York: Columbia University Press, 2020); Philip Coggan, *More: The 10,000 Year Rise of the World Economy* (London: Profile Books, 2020); Johan Norberg, *Open: The Story of Human Progress* (London: Atlantic Books, 2020).

the US, principally revolving around tobacco, rice, sugar, and later cotton and coffee.[3]

While the slave trade was abolished by Britain in its colonies in 1807 and slavery itself in 1833, it lingered on in many countries well into the late 19th century. Only a massively destructive civil war (1861–1865) ended slavery in the US, at least formally. In Brazil, slavery was only formally abolished in 1888. As late as the last years of the 19th century and the first years of the 20th, King Leopold II of Belgium established the Belgian Congo as a personal fiefdom (in which he never set foot), ruthlessly appropriated land and natural resources from the local inhabitants or their leaders by force or deception, and enslaved or conscripted vast numbers of Congolese inhabitants in exploiting their natural resources, in particular the rubber industry. These policies are estimated to have resulted in the death of almost half the Congolese population over the course of his reign through murder, mutilation, starvation, or the importation of infectious diseases, leaving behind permanent scars that afflict the country to the present day.[4] Even today human trafficking (especially in the sex trade), child labour, and bonded labour remain significant problems in various parts of the world.[5] The cotton and sugar industries survive to this day in the US because massive

---

[3] Glenn Rogers, *A Brief History of World Slavery: What Happened, Why It Happened, and What We Should Do About It* (Abilene, Texas: Simpson & Brook, 2019); James Walvin, *A Short History of Slavery* (London: Penguin Books, 2007); Hugh Thomas, *The Slave Trade: The Story of the Atlantic Slave Trade, 1440–1870* (New York: Simon & Schuster, 1997); Herbert S. Klein, *The Atlantic Slave Trade* (New York: Cambridge University Press, 2010).

[4] Adam Hochschild, *King Leopold's Ghost: A Story of Greed, Terror, and Heroism in Colonial Africa* (Boston: Houghton Mifflin, 1998); David Van Reybrouck, *Congo: The Epic History of a People*, translated by Sam Garrett (London: Fourth Estate, 2014).

[5] David Batstone, *Not For Sale: The Return of the Global Slave Trade – and How We Can Fight It* (New York: HarperOne, 2010).

protectionism and subsidies have replaced the slave labour on which they once depended, and in turn deny many developing countries their comparative advantage in these industries.[6]

While in some cases the colonizing powers designated or chartered nominally privately owned companies as their colonizing agents, such as the British East India Company, the Dutch East India Company, the Dutch West Indies Company, the Hudson Bay Company, and the British South Africa Company, the line between private and public was indistinct and permeable, with these entities often dependent on monopoly privileges, subsidies, and trade protection by their colonial principals. These companies were in effect sovereign and trading companies combined in their designated territories, and, often by military force, bribery, or duplicity in dealing with local leaders and their subjects, land, natural resources, and conscripted labour were appropriated in a company's interests. A particularly egregious example of this form of the incestuous relationship between state and chartered company was the agitation by the British East India Company to open up the Chinese market to opium exports from India, resulting in the opium wars between Britain and China in the middle of the 19th century and the establishment of a British colonial outpost in Hong Kong as a settlement of the war, inaugurating China's "century of humiliation" that colours China's relations with the West to the present day. Almost a century earlier, in 1773, a tea tax on imports of tea from the British East India Company provoked the Boston Tea Party ("no taxation without representation"), followed shortly thereafter by the American War of Independence.[7]

---

[6]   Sven Beckert, *Empire of Cotton: A Global History* (New York: Alfred A. Knopf, 2014); Marc Aronson and Marina Budhos, *Sugar Changed the World: A Story of Magic, Spice, Slavery, Freedom, and Science* (Boston: Clarion Books, 2010).

[7]   Stephen Bown, *Merchant Kings: When Companies Ruled the World* (Vancouver: Douglas & McIntyre, 2009); William Dalrymple,

Even the American-owned United Fruit Company, a near monopoly on the banana industry in Central America in the first half of the 20th century (and a monopsony in its deliberately segregated work force), while not nominally an agent of the US government, successfully enlisted the assistance of the US CIA as recently as 1954 to depose by coup a democratically elected government in Guatemala that sought to expropriate some of its unused land, further destabilizing the region (hence the genesis of the term "banana republic").[8]

Many of these historical manifestations of international trade and investment were neither free nor fair on most conceptions of "free" and "fair".

D)   THE EVOLUTION OF TRADE THEORY IN THE BOOKS

Amongst ancient Greek and Roman scholars, opinion was divided on the virtues of international trade. Some viewed such trade as risking corruption of local, social, and cultural values by contact with foreign merchants (merchants were generally viewed as of interior status). Others, in contrast, saw the unequal distribution of resources across the world by God (or Providence) as an inducement to bring together in peaceful harmony the various strands of humanity through trade (a view taken up in the Middle Ages by natural law scholars such as Grotius and later still by 19th-century liberals like John Stuart Mill, who saw cross-cultural engagement – a form

---

The Anarchy: The Relentless Rise of the East India Company (London: Bloomsbury, 2019).

[8]   Jason M. Colby, *The Business Empire: United Fruit, Race, and U.S. Expansion in Central America* (Ithaca: Cornell University Press, 2011).

of cosmopolitanism – as mutually beneficial beyond the material benefits of trade).[9]

In the Middle Ages, a distinctively economic perspective on trade emerged amongst scholars espousing various forms of mercantilism, where trade was seen as advantageous only if it led to an excess of exports over imports and hence generated a surplus of monetary specie to finance military engagements or to meet local credit needs. Alternatively, restricting imports, especially manufactured goods, was seen as a strategy for promoting local industry and employment. These views in turn were challenged by classical economists, in particular Adam Smith (1776) and David Ricardo (1817), who stressed the gains from the division of labour and specialization which were only limited by the extent of the market. Reflecting the intuition underlying these theories, we see the gains from specialization played out in our everyday lives today. Lawyers should not also attempt to provide their own plumbing, electrical, auto repair, dental, and medical services. Conversely, those who provide these services should not attempt to be their own lawyers. In small rural communities, even in developed countries, the range of specialized goods and services available to residents is often quite limited. But moving to large urban centres in the same countries renders a veritable cornucopia of specialized goods and services available to their residents. Expanding one's horizons from small rural communities to large urban centres, then to countries, and then to the world at large, often now facilitated by the internet and online shopping, vastly expands again the range of specialized goods and services available to many of the world's citizens.[10] Today, gains from trade are a fundamental

---

[9]   Douglas Irwin, *Against the Tide: An Intellectual History of Free Trade* (Princeton: Princeton University Press, 1996).

[10]   Fred Hochberg, *Trade Is Not a Four Letter Word: How Six Everyday Products Make the Case for Trade* (New York: Avid Reader Press/Simon & Schuster, 2020).

pillar of the world's prosperity, accounting for one quarter of world income. While trade restrictions result in income losses for all countries, it is important to note that smaller countries are more trade-dependent in terms of both imports and exports than larger ones. As such, small, open economies bear more costs from trade protectionism.[11]

While Smith's case for liberal international trade turned on exploitation of absolute advantages, Ricardo demonstrated that the scope for trade was much broader by emphasizing comparative rather than absolute advantage. Hence in his famous example, in which Portugal enjoyed an absolute advantage over England in producing both wine and cloth, its comparative advantage was larger in wine than cloth and England's comparative disadvantage smaller in cloth than wine: hence mutual gains from trade could be realized by Portugal exporting wine to England and importing cloth (and vice versa). A homely example helps illustrate this point: a lawyer can type a legal document faster than her secretary – in one hour rather than two – but the lawyer charges $300 per hour for services to clients while the secretary is paid $30 per hour. Both of them gain by the lawyer paying the secretary $60 for two hours' work and selling to clients for $300 the hour she saved from typing the document herself.

However, the writings of the classical economists were largely static in nature, and made little attempt to relate these models to actual trading patterns on the ground or the historical determinants of these patterns of comparative advantage (although Smith decried the vices of slavery and trading monopolies). In an equally and perhaps more important sense, these idealized or stylized models of cross-border trade were static, looking not only backwards, but also forwards. In a contemporary setting, where slavery and conquests by force

---

[11] Ralph Ossa, "The Costs of a Trade War" in Meredith A. Crowley, ed., *Trade War: The Clash of Economic Systems Endangering Global Prosperity* (London: CEPR Press, 2019).

have been largely ruled out (Russia's invasion of Crimea notwithstanding), what set of factors or determinants, including government policies, is likely to shape a country's comparative advantage going forward? For example, in Ricardo's example of Portugal trading wine for English cloth, looking back one can ask why England had a comparative advantage in making cloth, given that at the time he wrote most of it was made from imported raw cotton from India (while England imposed high tariffs on imported cloth to protect its local industry), and why Portugal had a comparative advantage in producing wine when other major wine producing countries such as France, Italy, and Spain were left unaccounted for? Moreover, Britain no longer produces significant quantities of cloth, textiles, or clothing, and Portugal is no longer one of the world's major producers of wine. Both countries have over the ensuing two centuries evolved quite different patterns of comparative advantage.

Subsequent to Smith and Ricardo, trade economists have debated some of these more dynamic factors bearing on changing trade patterns, such as the case for reciprocity in trade liberalization rather than unilateral trade liberalization to resolve zero sum or beggar-my-neighbour impediments to trade liberalization; the case for special dispensations for developing countries from generally prevailing trade disciplines and the strategic manipulation of terms of trade with other countries (the ratio of import prices to export prices) through combinations of tariffs, export taxes, and subsidies, especially in concentrated industries where there may be first-mover advantages.[12] But the painful fact must be acknowledged that economists do not have any generally accepted theory of the determinants of long-term economic growth, which often reflect quite idiosyncratic combinations of factors specific to country, time, and context and are

---

[12]   Douglas A. Irwin, *Against the Tide*.

likely to encompass a wide range of policy domains such as infrastructure, health care, education, industrial policy, R & D, stable and well-functioning political, bureaucratic, and legal institutions, and so on. In short, trade policy is likely to be only one factor amongst many in determining a country's evolving comparative advantage.[13]

To underscore the importance of broadly conceived dynamic determinants of comparative advantage, the (perhaps apocryphal) story is often told of a World Bank mission visiting South Korea 40 or 50 years ago, observing that South Korea was a major producer of rice, and advising South Korean authorities that this was where their country's comparative advantage lay and that they should grow more and better rice. This advice, with the benefit of hindsight, would have been disastrously misconceived as South Korea over the ensuing years transformed its economy from a principally agricultural economy to an industrial powerhouse. Much could be said of other countries earlier in their histories, such as the US, which transformed itself over the past century and a half from a principally agricultural economy to a manufacturing and service powerhouse, initially in the 19th century behind high tariff walls, and China today, which over the past 30 years has transformed its economy from principally an agricultural and heavy industry economy to the manufacturing factory of the

---

[13] Dani Rodrik, *One Economics, Many Recipes: Globalization, Institutions, and Economic Growth* (Princeton: Princeton University Press, 2008); Charles Kenny, *Getting Better: Why Global Development Is Succeeding – and How We Can Improve the World Even More* (New York: Basic Books, 2011); Abhijit Banerjee and Esther Duflo, *Good Economics for Hard Times: Better Answers to our Biggest Problems* (London: Allen Lane, 2019); Banerjee and Duflo, "How Poverty Ends", *Foreign Affairs*, January–February 2020; Justin Lin, *The Quest for Prosperity: How Developing Economies Can Take Off* (Princeton: Princeton University Press, 2012).

world, again reflecting a complex mix of market forces and state-directed policies.

These transformations (and many others) highlight the importance of focusing on factors, including government policies, that may transform the nature of a country's comparative advantages or disadvantages over time, and, crucially, on which of these are legitimate or illegitimate forces or determinants of changes in evolving trading patterns and relationships. This issue lies at the heart of contemporary free trade–fair trade debates and the fault-lines that these reflect.

II. Why trade agreements at all?[1]

Trade agreements between states have an ancient genesis –
a commercial treaty between the Kings of Egypt and Babylonia
to reduce tolls on trade between them existed in 2500 BC.
Much more recently, Britain's unilateral repeal of the Corn
Law in 1846 precipitated a series of trade treaties between
European states, beginning with the Cobden–Chevalier Treaty
between Britain and France in 1860, followed by French
treaties with the Zollverein, the German Customs Union, and
other European states, typically containing a Most Favoured
Nation clause under which countries agreed to extend to each
other any more favourable concessions each might subsequently negotiate with other countries. In 1868, the Rhine
was declared a free way for ships of all nations. However, the
heyday of trade-liberalizing treaties was relatively brief and
many European countries retreated from free trade following
a severe and sustained recession in the 1870s and subsequent
espousal of infant industry protection policies by Germany
and other states. The outbreak of World War I, followed by
the Great Depression, led to the collapse of world trade and the
rise of economic nationalism, epitomized by the enactment by
the US of the Smoot–Hawley Tariffs in 1930, raising duties on
many imports to 60 percent and provoking retaliatory tariffs
by other countries, the collapse of the gold standard, and

---

[1]   Michael J. Trebilcock and Joel Trachtman, *Advanced
Introduction to International Trade Law*, 2nd edn (Cheltenham:
Edward Elgar Publishing, 2020), Chapter 1.

competitive currency devaluations. In 1934 the US Congress enacted the *Reciprocal Trade Agreements Act*, which authorized the Administration to negotiate trade-liberalizing agreements on a bilateral basis, resulting in 31 such agreements in ensuing years. However, the outbreak of World War II again devastated world trade and brought an end to such efforts.[2]

A variety of economic and political rationales for trade agreements have been advanced.[3] A compelling political economy argument for such agreements is that they enable countries to enlist export-oriented industries, through improved access to foreign markets, as a counterweight to domestic political constituencies in import-impacted industries through the reciprocal exchange of binding trade concessions or commitments with other countries. Including these commitments in international treaties, which are not easily revoked, provides security and certainty (credible commitments) to investors and consumers who will be shielded, to some extent, from the shifting winds of domestic politics (a form of hands-tying strategy), and help resolve terms-of-trade driven problems in international trading relationships where major trading powers engage in mutually destructive, beggar-my-neighbour zero sum trade policies.[4]

Such agreements historically have also been sensitive to the fact that while international trade is a positive sum game on balance for countries that engage in it, typically there are also losers from trade liberalization commitments whose domestic political opposition needs to be mitigated if broadly social

---

[2]   Michael Trebilcock, Robert Howse, and Antonia Eliason, *The Regulation of International Trade*, 4th edn (Abingdon: Routledge, 2013), Chapter 1.

[3]   Douglas A. Irwin, Petros Mavroidis, and Alan Sykes, *The Genesis of the GATT* (New York: Cambridge University Press, 2008), Chapter 3.

[4]   See Kyle Bagwell and Robert Staiger, *The Economics of the World Trading System* (Cambridge, MA: MIT Press, 2002).

welfare-enhancing trade liberalization policies are not to be undermined. Hence, for example, the General Agreement on Tariffs and Trade (the GATT) from its inception in 1947 sought to mitigate adjustment costs from increased international trade through three mechanisms. First, gradualism, whereby tariff concessions were phased in over extended periods of time both within and across successive negotiating rounds, so that over the intervening period tariffs on industrial products have fallen worldwide from close to 50 percent in 1947 to under 5 percent on average today. Second, reciprocity, where, as noted above, export interests could be enlisted as a political counterweight to import-impacted sectors and adjustment costs in the latter mitigated over time as resources and jobs migrated from contracting import-impacted sectors to expanding export-oriented sectors. Third, reversibility, where, under various safeguard provisions (in effect *force majeure* provisions), trade restrictions could be temporarily reinstated to mitigate the impact of unforeseen import surges on domestic industries and their workforces even though such measures are often very costly to consumers relative to the value of jobs saved. None of these three factors are captured in the case for unilateral trade liberalization espoused by the classical economists. Clearly unilateral trade liberalization is better than autarky, but reciprocal trade liberalization is better still than unilateral trade liberalization in realizing potential gains from trade in both import and export sectors.

III. The case for multilateral trade agreements versus preferential agreements and special dispensations for developing countries[1]

A) THE CASE FOR MULTILATERALISM: THE NON-DISCRIMINATION PRINCIPLE

The architects of the Bretton Woods Agreement in 1944, in contemplating a new post-war international economic architecture, proposed the formation of the International Trade Organization to oversee a new multilateral system of liberalized international trade. However, the ITO never came into existence due to opposition to it in the US Congress, reflecting concerns that it would encroach excessively on domestic sovereignty. Instead, a provisional agreement negotiated in 1947 amongst 23 major trading countries as a prelude to the ITO (the GATT) became by default the institutional basis for the post-World War trade regime, and has evolved over time into

---

[1]   Michael J. Trebilcock and Joel Trachtman, *Advanced Introduction to International Trade Law*, Chapter 1.

the World Trade Organization, created in 1995, now comprising more than 160 member nations.[2]

Under the GATT, nine rounds of negotiations have now been undertaken. The first six of these rounds, up to and including the Kennedy Round which concluded in 1967, focused mainly on reciprocal reduction in tariffs on manufactured goods and to a much lesser extent agricultural products (which remain heavily protected today in many developed countries). More recent rounds, including the Tokyo Round ending in 1979 and the Uruguay Round ending in 1993, have increasingly focused on non-tariff barriers to trade. The current Doha Round, which was launched in 2001, appears to have largely petered out without substantial progress on any of the key negotiating issues (apart from a Trade Facilitation Agreement designed to streamline customs administration). This in part no doubt reflected the increasing entrenchment of the so-called Consensus Principle among member countries, which requires that no new commitments can be adopted without the consensus of all member states (i.e., lack of explicit objections by any single member state).

A key feature of the multilateral trading regime from the outset has been its adoption of the principle of non-discrimination, enshrined in two doctrines: the Most Favoured Nation Principle and the National Treatment principle. The Most Favoured Nation Principle, set out in Article I of the GATT, requires that any advantage, favour, privilege, or immunity granted by any member country to any product originating in or destined for any other country shall be accorded immediately and unconditionally to the like product originating in or destined for the territories of all other member countries. The centrality of the MFN principle to the multilateral system reflected both geopolitical and economic considerations that

---

[2] Petros Mavroidis, *The Regulation of International Trade* (2 vols) (Cambridge, MA: MIT Press, 2016).

the architects of the Bretton Woods Agreement viewed as central to the post-war international economic order. From a geopolitical point of view, the idea that all countries in the world, in principle, should be able to trade with each other under a common set of ground rules was seen as an important counterweight to the economic factionalism that characterized the inter-war years and that was widely seen as contributing to the outbreak of World War II.[3] From an economic perspective, a set of common ground rules were seen as most consistent with the full play of theories of comparative advantage, in that trade flows would be dictated by underlying relative efficiencies, rather than *sui generis* rules that structured each bilateral trading relationship. The MFN principle was complemented from the outset by the National Treatment principle, set out in Article III, which Article I incorporates and which prohibits countries from adopting internal taxes or regulations that treat domestic producers more favourably than foreign producers of like products (a source of many formal GATT/ WTO disputes over its interpretation and application as well as its relationship with Article XX, which provides general exceptions to GATT obligations).

While in many respects a noble vision, major derogations from the MFN principle were recognized from the outset in the case of bilateral or regional free trade agreements and customs unions subject to certain conditions set out in Article XXIV of the GATT, which were never strictly enforced, and subsequently by dispensations provided to the rapidly increasing number of recently independent developing country members of the GATT. On the import side these dispensations permitted unilateral trade restrictions to promote infant industries and to address balance-of-payments problems (1955), and on the export side they exhorted developed countries to provide

---

[3]   Jeffry A. Frieden, *Global Capitalism: Its Fall and Rise in the Twentieth Century* (New York: W.W. Norton & Co., 2006).

unilateral, non-reciprocal trade preferences to developing countries with respect to products of actual or potential export interest to them (1965).

B)   PREFERENTIAL TRADE AGREEMENTS

The exception for free trade areas and customs unions has proven particularly salient in permitting the proliferation of such arrangements from the early 1990s onwards (up from about 100 in 1990 to nearly 400 today). In 1990, GATT/WTO members had an average of two preferential trade agreement partners. This has increased to almost 13 over the past two decades or so.

The literature debating the merits and disadvantages of PTAs is wide ranging and contentious.[4] Three central issues dominate debates relating to the welfare effects of PTAs: 1) Are PTAs trade-creating or trade-diverting, given that they are inherently discriminatory in favour of members and against non-members? 2) Does the proliferation of PTAs and their *sui generis* rules increase transaction costs of international trade, especially for smaller firms, and thus inhibit trade? 3) How does the proliferation of PTAs affect the future course of international trade liberalization more generally and the roles and scope of these agreements relative to the multilateral regime?

The WTO, in a review in 2011 of the evidence on trade creation and diversion in PTAs, found that although the empirical evidence is not conclusive, PTAs are likely to create more trade among members and while trade diversion from more efficient non-members may play a role in some agreements and in some sectors, it is not the key effect of most preferential

---

[4]   Kyle Bagwell and Petros Mavroidis (eds), *Preferential Trade Agreements: A Law and Economic Analysis* (Cambridge: Cambridge University Press, 2011).

trade agreements.[5] As to the transaction costs for firms engaging in trade with other countries governed by *sui generis* trade rules including often complex and somewhat arbitrary rules of origin, Bhagwati likens the global web of PTAs to a "spaghetti bowl" that adds substantial complexity and transaction costs to international trade.[6] However, other authors argue that the scale of these transaction costs is constrained by virtue of the fact that producers always have the option of exporting under the MFN tariff rate, meaning that at worst the spaghetti bowl cannot diminish welfare beyond the original MFN starting point. As to the dynamic effects of PTAs on the international trading system at large, views widely differ as to whether they are building blocks or stumbling blocks to freer international trade in the long run. Some authors argue that PTAs offer the potential for deeper and broader liberalization, given that negotiations occur within or among smaller numbers of parties and that PTAs enable countries to advance the liberalization agenda into new issue areas and in this respect may function as laboratories of integration, serving as a pathfinder for possible future multilateral disciplines. Other authors argue that the WTO multilateral system performs functions in promoting freer international trade that PTAs can never replicate and may in some cases undermine,[7] and indeed that PTAs between small and large economies may reflect unequal bargaining power that coalition bargaining in the multilateral system can mitigate.

The current paralysis in the multilateral regime no doubt partly explains the recent proliferation of PTAs and presents

---

[5]   World Trade Organization, *World Trade Report* (Geneva: World Trade Organization, 2011).

[6]   Jagdish Bhagwati, *Termites in the Trading System: How Preferential Trade Agreements Undermine Free Trade* (Oxford: Oxford University Press, 2008).

[7]   Kyle Bagwell, Chad Bown, and Robert Staiger, "Is the WTO Passé?" (2016) 54 *Journal of Economic Literature* 1125.

major challenges if multilateralism is to continue to play a central role in the international trading system. In the multilateral regime, various supra-majority voting rules have been adopted with respect to the incorporation of new rules or amendments or official interpretations of existing rules. However, as noted above, a convention has developed over the past several decades that no major changes to the regime can occur without a consensus of all member states. While commendably egalitarian and democratic in some respects, consensus in recent years has proven elusive on many issues. Proposals to move to simple majority voting are unacceptable to major trading countries who resist the prospect of being out-voted by a majority of small economies. Alternative proposals to adopt some form of trade-weighted voting regime is unattractive to smaller countries who resist the prospect of being out-voted by a small number of large economies. This in turn has placed a disproportionate burden on the dispute resolution processes in the multilateral regime in resolving trade conflicts. This has led in turn to criticisms of the dispute settlement regime, especially the role of the Appellate Body, particularly by the US, for venturing beyond its role of interpreting and applying existing rules to more expansive forms of judicial lawmaking in contexts where existing rules are ambiguous or silent. Hence, the US is currently refusing to support the new appointments to the Appellate Body, which has ceased to function. Thus, dysfunctions in the operation of both the political and quasi-judicial organs of multilateral/ WTO trade regime have, at least for the time being, rendered preferential trade agreements the only feasible alternative negotiating fora.

C)   SPECIAL AND DIFFERENTIAL TREATMENT FOR DEVELOPING COUNTRIES

The special dispensations granted to developing countries from GATT disciplines (often referred to as Special and Differential Treatment) have been almost as controversial as the proliferation of PTAs.[8] Early in the history of the GATT, many developing countries, and indeed many mainstream development economists in developed countries and international agencies, argued that developing countries had often inherited truncated economies from their colonial overseers, where they had been largely restricted economically to the role of "hewers of wood and drawers of water", leaving them with large, traditional, and inefficient agricultural sectors. As with most developed countries earlier in their histories, a major transformation was called for in reallocating resources from traditional agricultural sectors to industrial or manufacturing sectors, reflecting dynamic rather than static conceptions of comparative advantage.[9] To facilitate and encourage this it was argued that at least temporary protectionism was required for these fledgling manufacturing industries in order to enable them to achieve minimum efficient scale and become competitive in both domestic and export markets. However, subsequent research has found that import substitution policies were often not achieving their goals and led to more or less

---

[8]   Chantal Thomas and Joel Trachtman, eds, *Developing Countries in the WTO Legal System* (Oxford: Oxford University Press, 2009).

[9]   Joseph Stiglitz, *Making Globalization Work* (New York: W.W. Norton & Co., 2006); Ha-Joon Chang, *Bad Samaritans: The Myth of Free Trade and the Secret History of Capitalism* (New York: Bloomsbury Press, 2008); Justin Lin, *The Quest for Prosperity*; Eric Reinert, *How Rich Countries Got Rich and Why Poor Countries Stay Poor* (New York: Public Affairs, 2008).

indefinite support for high cost, inefficient manufacturing industries and the rise of rent seeking behaviour and corruption that accompanied highly discretionary protectionist trade policies and related policies such as foreign exchange controls. These findings are often contrasted with the trade policies pursued by the so-called East Asian high growth economies (and some other developing economies) that have pursued policies of export-led growth (outward-oriented rather than inward-oriented policies), although it should be acknowledged that there is unresolved controversy as to the extent to which this export-led growth has been promoted by interventionist trade and related industrial policies designed to protect infant industries in their early stages and then subsequently to draw on them as a platform to support selective export-oriented industries.[10]

It should also be acknowledged that many poorer developing countries continue to rely on custom duties (tariffs) and export taxes as major sources of government revenue, especially the case for countries with large informal sectors that present major administrative challenges for internal tax regimes. Even developed countries earlier in their history relied heavily on customs duties as a major source of government revenue and did not adopt income taxes until early in the 20th century, often at the outset as a provisional measure to underwrite military expenditures in World War I.

On the export dimension of special and differential treatment, that is, nonreciprocal trade preferences, recent research suggests that they have not proved as valuable to developing countries as many had hoped. First, the benefits of the prefer-

---

[10]   Richard Baldwin, *The Great Convergence*; Steven Radelet, *The Great Surge: The Ascent of the Developing World* (New York: Simon & Schuster, 2015); Arvind Panagariya, *Free Trade and Prosperity: How Openness Helps the Developing Countries Grow Richer and Combat Poverty* (Oxford: Oxford University Press, 2019).

ences seem to be concentrated on the more advanced developing countries who have needed them least. Second, these preferences have tended to become less valuable over time as margins of preference have been eroded through reductions in MFN tariff levels. Third, preferences have often proven not to be durable, since they are often tied to the level of a country's economic development. Fourth, donor countries often reserve the right to withdraw preferences if imports become too competitive with domestic products. Finally, many import-sensitive products of major export interest to developing countries have been excluded from these preferential schemes.

An over-arching issue with respect to these special dispensations for developing countries is that no attempt was made in the GATT/WTO regime to define "developing countries", and indeed, the binary classification of all countries in the world as either "developed" or "developing" is obviously crude and simplistic – China is not Sierra Leone, India is not Bolivia, South Africa is not Haiti, and Haiti is not Costa Rica: more refined criteria for which countries should qualify for these dispensations have never been articulated.[11]

In summary, while an overwhelming consensus of professional economists favours free trade, there is much less consensus as to whether this is facilitated by trade agreements, and in particular whether it is most effectively facilitated through the multilateral trading regime or bilateral or regional preferential trade agreements. Moreover, the second major derogation from the MFN principle – special and differential treatment for developing countries – has proven almost as controversial as the PTA exception.

---

[11]   Hans Rosling, with Ola Rosling and Anna Rosling Rönnlund, *Factfulness: Ten Reasons We're Wrong about the World – and Why Things Are Better than You Think* (New York: Flatiron Books, 2018); Michael Trebilcock, "Between Universalism and Relativism" (2016) 66 *University of Toronto Law Journal* 330.

IV. The scope of trade agreements[1]

However these foregoing issues are resolved, another set of controversies relates to the appropriate scope of trade agreements or broader economic integration agreements. Historically, the focus of the GATT was on international trade in goods, and as noted above, the first six negotiating rounds under the GATT focused overwhelmingly on reducing tariffs and other border restrictions, such as quotas, relating to goods. More recent multilateral negotiations have focused on non-tariff barriers to trade (NTBs), which have proven much more contentious. In this respect, it is often argued that divergences or incompatibilities across a wide range of domestic regulatory and related policies create frictions in cross-border trade and hence are a significant impediment to it. Thus, the Uruguay Round focused on impediments to trade arising from divergent food safety standards and other technical standards; divergent domestic regulations pertaining to cross-border trade in services; harmonizing intellectual property standards to largely western norms; prohibiting discrimination in the treatment of foreign direct investment; and restricting discrimination in government procurement.

However, as Rodrik has persuasively argued, pursuing high levels of regulatory harmonization in such areas poses major challenges to the rationales for nation states and democratic decision-making on a wide range of domestic policy issues

---

[1]   Michael J. Trebilcock and Joel Trachtman, *Advanced Introduction to International Trade Law*, Chapter 1.

within such states.[2] Thus, it is difficult to sustain the position that the more regulatory harmonization the better without threatening the integrity of nation states and the legitimacy of domestic democratic decision-making. Thus, not surprisingly, attempts at achieving some minimum level of harmonization in most of the areas noted above have led to major controversies. Some PTAs have gone farther, and sought to either harmonize or stipulate minimum standards in areas such as labour standards, basic human rights more generally, and environmental standards, again generating predictable controversies over whether international trade or economic integration regimes that aspire to reducing non-tariff barriers to trade resulting from regulatory policy diversity are an unacceptable intrusion on national political sovereignty. This raises issues that sharply divide economists (as with other commentators), with some economists arguing for a more modest scope for international trade and economic integration agreements, while others argue that in a world with relatively low tariffs, non-tariff barriers to trade are the principal impediment to globally welfare-enhancing freer international trade. Indeed, an ambitious globalization agenda would take equally seriously the so-called four economic freedoms enshrined in the EU: cross-border movement of goods, services, capital, and people.

---

[2]   Dani Rodrik, *The Globalization Paradox: Democracy and the Future of the Work Economy* (New York: W.W. Norton & Co., 2011); Dani Rodrik, *Straight Talk on Trade: Ideas for a Sane World Economy* (Princeton, NJ: Princeton University Press, 2017); Michael Trebilcock and Robert Howse, "Trade Liberalization and Regulatory Diversity: Reconciling Competitive Markets with Competitive Politics" (1998) 6 *European Journal of Law and Economics* 5; for a critique of Rodrik's argument, see Joel Trachtman, "Review Essay: The Antiglobalization Paradox: Freedom to Enter into Binding International Law is Real Freedom" (2013) 36 *The World Economy* 1.

Liberalizing cross-border trade in services poses major problems, in that services are not subject to tariffs but tend to be regulated, sector-by-sector, profession-by-profession, or occupation-by-occupation in many countries, often at the sub-national level in the case of federal states and often by delegated self-regulatory bodies, so that the challenges of harmonizing regulatory standards or agreeing on minimum standards are immense, as slow progress in liberalizing service markets under the General Agreement on Trade in Services (GATS) negotiated during the Uruguay Round has underscored. Moreover, in the case of some classes of services, particularly financial services, the global financial crisis of 2007–2008 and the cross-border contagion effects that it exemplified has raised fundamental concerns over the appropriate regulation of financial markets both within countries and across borders.

With respect to cross-border movement of capital more generally, legitimate concerns have been raised about the effect of short-term or portfolio cross-border capital flows in destabilizing recipient countries' macroeconomic policies by inducing rapid asset appreciation, higher inflation and interest rates, and appreciation of the domestic currency, with converse effects in the event that these short-run capital flows are suddenly reversed. With respect to longer-term foreign direct investment, legitimate concerns arise on both sides of this relationship. Foreign direct investors are often concerned that once major investments have been sunk in a host country, they are susceptible to hold-up by host country governments through opportunistically changing the fiscal or regulatory environment, while host countries are predictably concerned about being drawn into bidding wars to attract and retain foreign direct investment and being induced to relax prevailing and legitimate regulatory or fiscal policies in this bidding process. Hence, the proliferation of bilateral investment treaties (up from 400 in 1990 to more than 3,000 today) has engendered vigorous controversies over whether an appropriate balance has been struck between the interests of foreign investors and the interests of host countries and their citizens.

Finally, with respect to the free movement of people across borders, very few countries, at least formally, permit free movement of people across their borders, with the prominent exception of the European Union, which enshrines the right of free movement of citizens and permanent residents amongst its member states. The economic evidence suggests that reasonably open immigration policies are generally welfare-enhancing, in an economic sense, for recipient countries, with perhaps an exception in the case of the least skilled domestic workers competing with immigrants for jobs, and obviously welfare-enhancing for most immigrants.[3] However, free cross-border movement of people has proven vastly more controversial than any of the other three freedoms: it appears in large part to explain the Brexit vote in the UK referendum in June 2016 and was central to many of the Trump Administration's policies designed to radically reduce immigration in general and to restrict certain classes of immigrants in particular.

Hence, once the focus shifts from the case for trade agreements in general, and from the more particular issues raised by the case for and against multilateral versus preferential bilateral trade agreements and special trading arrangements for developing countries, the scope of international trade and broader economic integration agreements becomes intensely controversial, not only amongst commentators and interested or affected citizens generally, but amongst economists as well. Thus, the initial overwhelming consensus amongst

---

[3]   Michael Trebilcock, *Dealing with Losers: The Political Economy of Policy Transitions* (Oxford: Oxford University Press, 2014), Chapter 7; George J. Borjas, *We Wanted Workers: Unraveling the Immigration Narrative* (New York: W.W. Norton & Company, 2016).

economists in favour of free trade provides limited insight once one turns to the appropriate scope and particularities of these agreements.

V. Contemporary unfair trade claims[1]

It is commonly argued that some forms of contemporary international trade may constitute a form of unfair trade or unfair competition, and hence economic dislocations induced by unfair trade may be normatively unacceptable. I review many of these claims below.

A) PERSISTENT TRADE DEFICITS

Persistent trade deficits are often cited as evidence of unbalanced trade commitments, the large and persistent trade deficit that the US runs with China being the most prominent contemporary example. However, as many economists have pointed out, bilateral trade deficits are ubiquitous in domestic economies. For example, I pay money to my dentist for her services but she does not buy any of my books. Similarly, I often buy dinner at a local restaurant but the owner never buys any of my books or my consulting services. However, in both cases, they buy other goods and services across the economy, and in turn the providers of these goods and services may buy my books (or their children in the case of students) or my consulting services.

Moreover, in an international trade context, as Irwin points out, if a foreign country is exporting more than it imports from another country, the overall balance of payments is divided

---

[1]   See generally, Michael J. Trebilcock and Joel Trachtman, *Advanced Introduction to International Trade Law*.

between the current account and the financial account, which includes all portfolio and direct investments. Foreign countries can either use their export earnings to purchase imports or invest the surplus in acquiring assets or investments in the country with which they are running a trade surplus (e.g., China's investment in US treasury bills and other securities). According to Irwin:

> If the US took action to reduce the trade deficit in an effort to reduce the number of jobs lost to imports, then capital inflows from abroad would necessarily have to fall (i.e. foreign investors would no longer buy treasury bills and the dollar would depreciate). Thus, domestic investment would have to be financed by domestic savings, implying higher interest rates, which would reduce the number of jobs created by business investment. In the end, the positive impact of a lower trade deficit on employment might be offset by the negative impact of lower domestic investment and higher interest rates.[2]

Persistent global trade deficits may raise more complex issues. Of course, persistent trade deficits may be partly symptomatic of some of the phenomena discussed below – for example, currency manipulation, subsidies, forced technology transfers and so on – but these should be addressed on their own terms. More generally, persistent trade deficits may provide support, at least politically, for more substantive reciprocity (symmetry) in market access in terms of tariff levels, sectors open to foreign direct investment and conditions relating thereto, subsidies and so on, ideally on an MFN basis. This approach seems strongly preferable to bilateral trade arrangements, extracted under threat of trade sanctions, whereby trade surplus countries commit to increasing purchases of goods or services of certain categories in certain amounts from trade deficit countries, often at the expense of third countries that are more efficient producers of the goods or services in ques-

---

[2]   Douglas Irwin, *Free Trade Under Fire*, at 145, 146.

tion. The so-called Phase 1 trade agreement between the US and China in January 2020 exhibits some of these features and reflects a form of managed trade, not free trade,[3] as discussed in a later section of this book.

B)   CURRENCY MANIPULATION

The intricate relationship between trade and exchange rates raises a series of concerns over the practice of currency manipulation in world trade. It is often claimed that some governments deliberately manipulate their currency to induce an undervaluation and hence render their exports cheaper and imports more costly. Devaluation may risk retaliatory zero sum currency devaluations or other trade restrictive responses by affected trading partners, and also carries domestic costs in terms of higher costs of imports to consumers, and higher risks of domestic price inflation. Particularly in developing countries, a falling exchange rate could make essential items like imported medicines and food unaffordable. Hence, currency devaluation is not a risk-free strategy.[4]

Nevertheless, currency manipulation has provoked a long history of international conflicts and is a central point of contention in contemporary trade disputes, such as that between the US and China. The George W. Bush and Obama Administrations intermittently expressed concerns over China's exchange rate valuation, and pressured China to float its Renminbi. These concerns were based on a conception of a "fair" exchange rate as one that is based on currency markets. It was claimed that the Renminbi has been "unfairly" rigged to keep Chinese exports artificially cheap. Following

---

    [3]   For further discussion of trade deficits, see James McBride and Andrew Chatsky, "The US Trade Deficit: How Much Does It Really Matter?" *US Council on Foreign Relations*, March 8, 2019.

    [4]   Michael J. Trebilcock, Robert Howse, and Antonia Eliason, *The Regulation of International Trade*, Chapter 6.

the election of President Trump, the issue of currency manipulation has been a focal point in the US administration's trade policy, as Trump had repeatedly labelled China, among other countries, as a currency manipulator. In any event, it now seems widely accepted that China has recently allowed its currency to appreciate significantly and that it may no longer be significantly undervalued.

Despite ongoing conflicts over currency manipulation in trade disputes, international trade law largely fails to provide adequate remedies. One possible legal solution that many commentators have looked to is the WTO's Agreement on Subsidies and Countervailing Measures (SCM), since currency devaluation is generally agreed to be the equivalent of an export subsidy. However, this avenue provides little prospect of success. Article 1.1 of the SCM states that the existence of a subsidy requires the measure to constitute either a financial contribution or a form of price support. These requirements are difficult to meet in the case of currency manipulations. Exchange rate policies mostly do not involve direct or potential transfers of economic resources from the government to private companies and thus do not constitute a financial contribution. Currency devaluations also cannot be considered price support because even though the result is a lower price of exports, it has the same effect on prices of these products in the domestic market, and thus does not create a difference between foreign and domestic market prices. Overall, despite their similar effects, it is difficult to classify currency measures as a form of subsidy under the SCM Agreement.[5]

GATT Article XV(4) is another possible route for legal action in response to currency devaluation. This article states that "contracting parties shall not, by exchange action, frustrate

---

[5] Nathan Fudge, "Walter Mitty and the Dragon: An Analysis of the Possibility for WTO or IMF Action against China's Manipulation of the Yuan" (2011) 45 *Journal of World Trade* 349.

the intent of the provisions of this Agreement".[6] However, the meanings of "frustrate" and "intent of the GATT" have not been clearly defined. The interpretive note of GATT Article XV(4) further indicates that a mere infringement of a particular GATT provision does not necessarily constitute the frustration of intent, as long as the infringement does not constitute an "appreciable departure from" the Article's intent. This interpretation leaves open the question of how to translate this standard into a concrete threshold, generating much ambiguity.[7]

A final possibility is to invoke the IMF. GATT Article XV(2) states that in the case of disputes between member countries involving exchange arrangements, GATT parties shall "consult fully with the IMF" and accept the IMF's determination as to whether a country's exchange arrangements are consistent with its obligations under the IMF Articles of Agreement.[8] This route of action links the GATT/WTO to the IMF, and would involve the examination of whether currency measures are consistent with IMF provisions. Article IV of the IMF Articles of Agreement prohibits the manipulation of exchange rates in order to obtain an unfair competitive advantage. However, there is a great deal of conceptual difficulty with this prohibition since IMF provisions do not define the terms "manipulation" and "unfair competitive advantage". The relevant standard of fairness has long been

---

6   Nathan Fudge, "Walter Mitty and the Dragon: An Analysis of the Possibility for WTO or IMF Action against China's Manipulation of the Yuan".

7   Bryan Mercurio and Celine Sze Ning Leung, "Is China a 'Currency Manipulator'? The Legitimacy of China's Exchange Regime Under the Current International Legal Framework" (2009) 43 *The International Lawyer* 1257.

8   Bradley Schield, "China's Exchange Rate Manipulation: What Should the United States Do?" (2012) 34 *Houston Journal of International Law* 415.

an issue of contention within the international community.[9] In a 2007 Executive Board decision, the IMF provided some interpretive guidance. Currency manipulation was defined as "policies that are targeted at – and actually affect – the level of an exchange rate". On the concept of unfair advantage, the decision stated that the determination of an unfair advantage requires the finding that the member engaged in currency manipulation policies for the purpose of securing fundamental exchange rate misalignment and that the purpose of securing such misalignment is to increase net exports. It further stated that "a touchstone for manipulation is an effort to influence the balance of trade" and that "any representation made by the member regarding the purpose of its policies will be given the benefit of any reasonable doubt". These requirements for the determination of currency manipulation, particularly the requirement that the purpose of the policies in question is to increase net exports, make it hard to officially label any country a currency manipulator since the country could always offer various alternative explanations of its motives. These alternative explanations are also given the benefit of any reasonable doubt. Even if a determination of currency manipulation has been established, the IMF lacks an effective enforcement mechanism. While the IMF provides that it would oversee the compliance of each member, the most likely modes of surveillance and enforcement are dialogue and persuasion. There has also been no suggestion that sanctions like curtailment of access to IMF resources, suspension, or expulsion from membership would enter the surveillance and enforcement process. The primary enforcement device of the IMF has been the cutting off of countries from IMF bor-

---

[9]   Michael J. Trebilcock, Robert Howse, and Antonia Eliason, *The Regulation of International Trade*, 4th ed.

rowings, but these mechanisms are of little force to countries that do not depend on IMF borrowings, such as China.[10]

Amidst these difficulties, some scholars have proposed that the IMF and WTO should cooperate to combat currency manipulation. Under this proposal, countries could file complaints under the WTO, and the WTO would ask the IMF to determine the existence of and extent of currency manipulation. After the IMF finds the existence of manipulation, the WTO would then authorize the complaining country to impose countermeasures. While this proposal reflects the intricately connected nature of trade and exchange policy, this proposal requires both the IMF and WTO to change their agreements. In the case of the WTO, this would require consensus, which is likely to be difficult since countries that desire more control over their currency would be reluctant to agree to more binding constraints. In addition, this proposal would effectively give the IMF the power to regulate all currencies, and even the US, the leading complainant, might not be willing to give up the sovereignty of its Federal Reserve to this extent.[11]

C)   DUMPING[12]

A common complaint by domestic producers in many importing countries is that foreign exporters to these countries are selling their goods in importing countries at lower prices than they typically sell such goods for in their home markets and, pursuant to enabling provisions that have existed in the GATT

---

[10]   Robert W. Staiger and Alan O. Sykes, "'Currency Manipulation' and World Trade" (2010) 9 *World Trade Review* 583.

[11]   Laurence Howard, "Chinese Currency Manipulation: Are There Any Solutions?" (2013) 27 *Emory International Law Review* 1215.

[12]   Michael J. Trebilcock and Joel Trachtman, *Advanced Introduction to International Trade Law*, Chapter 6.

since its inception, are entitled to levy antidumping duties on the imported products in the amount of the difference in prices prevailing in exporting and importing countries. Antidumping duties are now widely levied by many countries around the world (the US historically being the most prominent user).

From an economic perspective, it is difficult to identify a coherent rationale for most such duties. Firms in all kinds of markets, both domestic and international, face different competitive conditions in different markets and hence different levels of price sensitivity (price elasticity) in these markets. Cinema operators often charge children and seniors lower prices for seat tickets than most adults. Airlines charge business travellers higher prices than leisure travellers. In an international trade context, foreign exporters may face less competition in their home markets than in importing countries' markets, perhaps because of trade barriers, lax competition laws, or more established reputations, and hence must price more aggressively in the latter markets in order to be competitive, given the broader choices among suppliers that consumers face.

An alternative test of dumping often used turns on whether a foreign exporter is charging prices in importing countries below fixed and variable costs (average total cost). Such pricing strategies might be thought to be evidence of predatory pricing, that is, driving domestic and other foreign competitors out of importing countries' markets with a view to establishing monopolies and higher long-run prices. While this possibility cannot be rejected out of hand, for the most part it is not the test for predatory pricing applied to domestic competitors in countries' domestic competition or antitrust laws, which recognize that pricing below average total cost but above marginal cost may often be justified. This may be the case, for example, with new competitors seeking to establish a foothold in a market where consumers have no familiarity with their products, or in times of excess supply or reduced demand creating surpluses of products, especially perishable products, that need to be disposed of in a relatively short time frame. Hence, this test violates at least the spirit of the National Treatment principle by subjecting foreign firms to more severe pricing constraints than apply to domestic competitors.

A yet further test of dumping that is often used in the case of foreign exporters from countries that are deemed to be Non-Market Economies is whether prices charged by these exporters in importing countries' markets are lower than prices charged in surrogate third country markets, on the ground that prices and costs in Non-Market Economies are not determined by market forces but by various forms of state intervention. These surrogates are often arbitrarily or strategically chosen by domestic industries to inflate the margin of dumping for which they are seeking duties. Again, this has been a point of friction in recent trade conflicts between the US and China.

D) SUBSIDIES[13]

One of the most vexing issues in international trade law and policy is settling on an agreed set of ground rules for regulating the conferral of subsidies by governments on classes of activities, sectors, firms, or products where such subsidies may have adverse effects on the terms of trade with other countries. Subsidies may take many different forms beyond direct cash transfers and might take the form of special tax dispensations, provision by government of key inputs below market determined prices, access to credit on below market determined terms, favourable treatment in government procurement tendering, and so on. Such subsidies may confer advantages on firms that benefit from them in foreign export

---

[13] Michael J. Trebilcock and Joel Trachtman, *Advanced Introduction to International Trade Law*, Chapter 7.

markets, in third country markets where they are competing with firms from other countries, or in their own domestic markets where they are facing competition from foreign firms.

During the Uruguay Round negotiations of the GATT (1986 to 1995), a detailed Subsidies and Countervailing Measures Agreement (SCM Agreement) was negotiated that attempts to lay down detailed rules for permissible and impermissible subsidies and authorizes importing countries to impose unilateral countervailing duties on subsidized imports and, in the case of subsidies that affect the conditions of competition in third country markets or in the subsidizing country's own market, make a formal complaint to the WTO dispute settlement body which if upheld may result in retaliatory trade sanctions.

However, despite these efforts at clarifying the ground rules that regulate subsidies that may distort international trade, major disputes continue to break out between or amongst countries over subsidy issues. It is not difficult to see why. Almost all governments around the world subsidize, directly or indirectly, a wide range of activities ranging from healthcare to education, infrastructure, the administration of justice, R&D, and often, through intellectual property law, quite specific forms of innovation. Like currency manipulation, subsidies designed to enhance international competitiveness are not costless for governments and their citizens and must be financed directly or indirectly, which entails opportunity costs, and risks zero sum retaliatory actions by trading partners.

As Bown and Hillman usefully summarize in a recent paper, there are four main concerns with the WTO's subsidies regime. The first is a definitional concern regarding what constitutes a subsidy. Currently, only governments or public bodies are considered capable of providing subsidies. Importantly, this definition excludes state-owned enterprises (SOEs). Second, there is a high evidentiary burden to prove the existence of a prohibited subsidy. It is often difficult for complaining countries to provide adequate proof to establish that the entity giving subsidies is a public entity with governmental control or that a private entity's actions were directed by the government. It is also difficult to prove that a financial contribution confers a benefit by providing funds or resources at below market prices, and to prove that adverse effects were caused by the subsidies. Third, there is a chronically low rate of compliance with the obligation to notify subsidies to the WTO. Finally, there are serious issues with remedies. For prohibited subsidies, the remedy is to withdraw the subsidy without delay. For other subsidies, the remedy is either to impose CVDs or to commence a serious prejudice case at the WTO. For CVDs, they are available only in countries that import the product and have a domestic industry making similar goods: the imposition of CVDs also requires long and extensive investigation. And moreover, these duties may simply push the subsidized goods into other markets. For serious prejudice cases, WTO remedies are only prospective and do not redress past injury. Also, elements of proof have a temporal element, which means that serious prejudice cases cannot be brought until enough time has passed, allowing the subsidies to cause "displacement" or a "depression" in prices. In other words, the remedies are only available after the harm is done.[14]

Subsidy controversies have been at the heart of recent US–China trade conflicts, where it is often claimed that the complex and opaque interrelationships between the state at both national and local levels, the Communist Party, state-owned enterprises, and formal and informal networks of private enterprises and the state and its various emanations make it almost impossible to determine whether China's apparent comparative advantage in various areas

---

[14]   Chad P. Bown and Jennifer A. Hillman, "WTO'ing a Resolution to the China Subsidy Problem" (2019) 22 *JIEL* 557.

of international trade is a reflection of underlying relative efficiencies or contrived or artificial advantages conferred by state or Communist Party policies and agencies. These unique features have led Mark Wu to argue that China's rise presents the multilateral trade system with an unprecedented challenge because China's unique economic system, which he terms "China, Inc.", was unforeseen by WTO law or the terms of China's Accession in 2001, and the current WTO is thus ineffective in dealing with disputes involving China. Wu has identified six features that make "China, Inc." unique: First, the State-Owned Assets Supervision and Administration Commission, which allows the party-state to control major industries while at the same time relying to some extent on market signals; second, financial entities in China permit the party-state to control the largest banks and to direct financial resources; third, Chinese Communist Party (CCP) entities and state entities provide guidance across government agencies and firms; fourth, there are informal networks between entities that facilitate coordination; fifth, the CCP is able to set performance metrics and control personnel appointment for state-controlled firms, which incentivizes firm officials, board members, and managers to act in line with party interests; and sixth, there are formal and informal linkages between the CCP and private enterprises. Overall, these features combine to produce a unique economic system where the CCP can control the economy, while at the same time taking advantage of market mechanisms.[15]

China's unique economic system, with a combination of market and non-market elements, means that the Chinese party-state can deploy a range of policies that might have

---

[15] Mark Wu, "The 'China, Inc.' Challenge to Global Trade Governance", (2016) 57 *Harvard International Law Journal* 261. See also Branko Milanovic, *Capitalism Alone: The Future of the System that Rules the World* (Cambridge, MA: The Belknap Press of Harvard University Press, 2019), Chapter 3.

the economic effect of a subsidy, without falling within the WTO's definition. In particular, China's upstream SOEs often provide key inputs to downstream firms at below market prices, regardless of the level of market competition or privatization of the downstream part of the industry. One example is in the steel industry, where an upstream SOE provides hot rolled steel at subsidized prices to benefit downstream steel manufacturers in China. Another example is the provision of below market financing by state-owned banks to SOEs or private entrepreneurs. In general, the WTO regime on remedies provides little guidance in addressing concerns related to China's subsidies and SOEs.[16]

A further factor likely to intensify subsidy disputes in the future is the massive business bail-out policies adopted by many governments in the current coronavirus pandemic, which will provoke complaints that in many cases they are unfairly distorting comparative advantage in trading relationships.

In response to the deficiencies of the WTO's subsidies regime and the issues raised by the China, Inc. challenge, Bown and Hillman advance a number of proposals to improve the governance of subsidies. For example, there should be better information and analysis to measure, diagnose, and define the problem, and intensified efforts to create categories of permitted subsidies and a category of subsidies that distort production and trade. In light of the China, Inc. problem, the term "government or public body" should be redefined and broadened. In terms of evidentiary problems, rebuttable presumptions should be established to shift the burden of proof to the subsidizing member. On the notifications problem, administrative penalties should be imposed for the failure to notify subsidies to the WTO. Enforcement could be taken to

---

[16] Chad P. Bown and Jennifer A. Hillman, "WTO'ing a Resolution to the China Subsidy Problem".

the supranational level, allowing the WTO secretariat to bring cases of its own motion.[17]

In my view, more pragmatism and less self-righteousness are required in resolving these issues. After all, many currently developed countries (including the US) early in their economic development heavily protected, subsidized, or otherwise promoted emerging sectors of their economies, and continue to do so with respect to some sectors. Ratcheting down trade-distorting subsidies, locking serious non-trade related rationales, like past negotiated tariff reductions, may be the path of pragmatism.

E)   INTELLECTUAL PROPERTY RIGHTS[18]

Many countries, as they have moved along the economic development trajectory, have undergone major shifts in the structure of their economies, from primary reliance on agriculture and perhaps natural resources, to manufacturing, and then to services. With this process of evolution has come an increased prominence of various forms of intangible capital where ideas matter more than land or factories – a process likely to be accelerated in the future with technological innovations in artificial intelligence and related fields.[19] Thus, increasingly intense international competition has evolved for engrossing a comparative advantage or even a dominant position in these new technologies, presaging new domains of potential international conflict over appropriate ground rules

---

[17]   Chad P. Bown, Jennifer A. Hillman, "WTO'ing a Resolution to the China Subsidy Problem".

[18]   Michael J. Trebilcock and Joel Trachtman, *Advanced Introduction to International Trade Law*.

[19]   Jonathan Haskel and Stian Westlake, *Capitalism Without Capital: The Rise of the Intangible Economy* (Princeton: Princeton University Press, 2018).

for striking a balance between protecting intellectual property rights to incentivize innovation and providing appropriate access to the underlying ideas or technologies. In the course of the Uruguay Round of the GATT, the Trade-Related Intellectual Property Rights Agreement (TRIPS) was negotiated, which required all member states – with longer transition periods for developing countries – to adopt domestic intellectual property rights laws that reflected the minimum standards set out in TRIPS, which were essentially developed country and particularly US standards.

Profound controversy continues to surround the TRIPS Agreement in terms of whether it has struck an appropriate balance between technological innovation and technological diffusion. An early critique that attracted much worldwide attention was that intellectual property rights had been given excessive protection, and in particular were a serious impediment to poorer developing countries gaining effective access to essential medicines for treating the AIDS epidemic and other tropical diseases. Subsequent amendments to the TRIPS have allowed developing countries greater latitude to invoke the compulsory licensing provisions in the agreement to deal with national emergencies, including importing generic drugs from other countries when they lack their own manufacturing capacity upon payment of adequate remuneration to the patent-holder. While those amendments mitigate earlier concerns, the conditions are undefined and untested,[20] and the US continues to press for TRIPS-plus protection of intellectual property rights, especially for pharmaceuticals, in PTAs. As discussed later in this book, these concerns are already re-emerging in the context of the coronavirus pandemic, where new vaccines or antivirals may be subject to

---

[20]   Alan Sykes, "TRIPS, Pharmaceuticals, Developing Countries and the Doha Solution", (2002) 3 *Chicago Journal of International Law* 47.

patent rights in their developers, raising barriers to access, particularly for citizens in poorer developing countries.

A different set of concerns has recently emerged, where it is argued that foreign countries (again most prominently China) have encouraged the appropriation of the intellectual property of firms based in other countries either through lax domestic intellectual property laws or lax enforcement thereof (including cyber-piracy as a limiting example), hence conferring on them an artificial comparative advantage in international trade and unfairly prejudicing firms who developed the innovations, and their work forces.

Most economists acknowledge that there is no widely agreed methodology for determining the socially optimal length and breadth of intellectual property patent protection (i.e., the optimal trade-off between technological innovation and diffusion), which is likely to vary sharply by class of innovation and by country so that the minimum across-the-board standards prescribed by TRIPS will often be ill-adapted to widely divergent global contexts and hence provide fertile ground for ongoing conflicts, as exemplified by contemporary conflicts between the US and China over technology transfer.

In the case of China, there are two types of situation that lead to technology transfer. The first is when the transfer is compelled by administrative processes. Here, foreign firms are subject to administrative requirements, where the government forces foreign firms to disclose technical information including designs, formulas, and trade secrets in exchange for market access. Many firms allege that the information demanded by Chinese governmental agencies is unnecessary for legitimate regulatory purposes, and that this proprietary information ends up being shared with domestic Chinese firms. In addition, for foreign firms that have already invested in the country, they have no choice but to comply with these requirements because doing otherwise would mean losing their investments and their market access. These alleged practices violate China's legal obligations such as the TRIPS

Agreement, where China is obligated to protect undisclosed information submitted to government agencies, and their WTO commitment not to condition foreign investment approval on technology transfers. There have been efforts within China to reform its administrative requirements in response to these concerns. For example, in the new Foreign Investment Law, China prohibits administrative agencies from disclosing trade secrets of foreign investors.[21]

The second situation is when the technology transfer is the result of ownership restrictions on foreign investment, such as the joint venture (JV) requirement. This situation is more complex because unlike the first, it does not violate existing international trade law. For example, in the case of mandatory JV requirements, if a certain technology is necessary for the operation of the JV, the foreign owner must share the technology with its domestic partner, who might subsequently become a competitor. Another complicating factor is that the Chinese partner may be under government pressure to demand technologies from their foreign partner, since mandatory JVs must receive government approval. Thus, it is difficult to tell whether the demand for technology comes from the government or solely from the Chinese partner firm. In addition, foreign investment is banned outright in certain sectors, giving foreign firms no choice but to partner with Chinese firms by providing them with proprietary information in exchange for a share of the revenue.[22]

In the case of technology transfer via ownership restrictions, the problem of insufficient WTO regulation has large consequences. Technology transfer via mandatory JVs is currently not regulated under general principles of international

---

[21]   Julia Ya Qin, "Forced Technology Transfer and the US-China Trade War: Implications for International Economic Law" (2019) 22 *JIEL* 743.

[22]   Julia Ya Qin, "Forced Technology Transfer and the US-China Trade War: Implications for International Economic Law".

trade law, and is only constrained by specific undertakings in PTAs or GATS mode 3, which treat foreign ownership restrictions as a matter of market access subject to negotiation. In effect, technology transfer in this sense resembles a "market-for-technology" policy. The underlying normative debate concerns whether or not this market-for-technology exchange is a legitimate tool for economic and technological development. On the one hand, the prevailing Chinese view sees this exchange as fair, based on the assumption that market access is not a given. On the other hand, Western critics see this exchange as fundamentally unfair, based on the assumption that market access should be free from government intervention in the first place.

One promising argument put forward by Julia Ya Qin takes a middle road: the fairness of the market-for-technology exchange should not be answered in absolute terms, but depends on a country's level of technological and economic development.[23] However, this is an issue on which current international trade law provides no guidance: the GATT/WTO members never defined what they meant by a "developing country". Qin proposes that new regulations for technology transfer should begin with a country classification system based on a combination of income-based rankings and innovation indices. In China's case, for example, the market-for-technology policy was fair when it was first adopted four decades ago, at a time when the country was an economic and technological backwater. At that time, foreign technology transfer would benefit not only China but also foreign companies, as it led Chinese producers to become more efficient, and improved the efficiency of global supply chains led by Western firms. However, this policy is no longer fair in the current context since China is now able to

---

[23] Julia Ya Qin, "Forced Technology Transfer and the US-China Trade War: Implications for International Economic Law".

compete economically and technologically with others on an equal basis. In this context, government intervention in technology transfer would result in unfair advantages. As such, international regulation should differentiate between levels of economic and technological development of the technology receiving countries. Rather than an outright ban of the market-for-technology exchange, regulation should allow such policies if adopted by poor countries, while restricting these practices for countries with a high level of economic and technological capacity.

F)   FOREIGN DIRECT INVESTMENT[24]

As noted in an earlier section of this book, Bilateral Investment Treaties (BITS) have proliferated in recent years and have attracted much controversy. Typically, these treaties provide for a private right of action for monetary compensation by foreign direct investors who can demonstrate that policies adopted by host countries subsequent to their investment violate the National Treatment principle by treating them less favourably than domestic investors in like circumstances; or violate the principle of customary international law of fair and equitable treatment; or entail measures constituting expropriation or measures tantamount to expropriation in the treatment of their investments. Such claims are typically adjudicated by a panel of private arbitrators pursuant to arbitral regimes established by the World Bank or other international organizations. Many host countries, especially developing countries with fragile domestic legal systems, have viewed BITS as a strategy for attracting increased flows of FDI, although the empirical evidence on their efficacy in this respect is mixed,

---

[24]   Michael J. Trebilcock and Joel Trachtman, *Advanced Introduction to International Trade Law*, Chapter 11.

especially as more BITS are signed, implying diminishing marginal effects of each new treaty.

Criticisms of these regimes have focused on both substance and process. On substance, it is often argued that key provisions in these treaties such as fair and equitable treatment, or measures tantamount to expropriation, are vague or ambiguous and have attracted inconsistent interpretations and applications by different arbitral panels and are not subject to an effective appellate review process. On process, it is often argued that the proceedings of arbitral panels are not open and transparent and preclude participation by third-party constituencies in host countries whose interests are legitimately implicated in the matters in dispute. Moreover, it is often argued that private arbitrators are vulnerable to conflicts of interest in appearing as arbitrators in some cases and advocates in others and have a generalized interest in promoting a higher volume of cases that will engage their services.

These concerns are in many respects well taken, and argue for treating international investment disputes in the way international trade disputes have typically been treated, that is, state-to-state dispute resolution, with an appellate review process, and focusing centrally on the non-discrimination principle, that is, National Treatment, whereby foreign direct investors are required to be treated no less favourably than domestic investors in similar circumstances – no worse but no better as is often the case under BITS. The Trade-Related Investment Measures Agreement (TRIMS) negotiated during the Uruguay Round largely adopts this approach for post-establishment measures and has generated very few formal disputes – although perhaps in part reflecting the attractions to foreign investors of the BITS alternative. Such an agreement must necessarily leave room for negotiation over which sectors fall within its ambit and which sectors are closed, in whole or in part, to foreign direct investment (discussed further below in relation to national security considerations).

Beyond these issues, a glaring gap in international rules governing foreign direct investment is the almost complete lack of attention to disciplines on positive inducements for FDI as opposed to constraints on the regulation thereof. In recent years countries seeking to attract foreign direct invest-ment, and indeed subnational jurisdictions in federal states, often engage in bidding wars to attract FDI by offering grants, infrastructure investments, loans on preferential terms, tax holidays, or tax deferrals to attract foreign investors to their jurisdiction. This is often a zero sum game for governments (although not for foreign investors). However, at present there are few international constraints on this game.

In a rather similar vein, jurisdictions often engage in tax competition to attract the headquarters – often nominal – of multinational companies by offering low or nominal corporate tax rates, and in some cases functioning as literal tax havens. With the increasing prominence of intangible capital, as noted above, it is relatively easy for multinational companies to locate their nominal headquarters to any of a wide range of jurisdictions in order to minimize their tax liability. Again, as with subsidy wars to attract foreign investment, there are currently very few international disciplines or effective forms of international coordination in constraining this tax-driven jurisdiction shopping. This may have a dramatic negative effect on a country's revenue raising capacity, and hence ability to finance a wide variety of public goods, including infrastructure, healthcare, education and active labour market policies.[25]

More debatably perhaps, the proliferation of Special Economic Zones or Export Processing Zones in many coun-tries, typically entailing dispensations from fiscal or regu-latory policies that obtain more generally in such countries,

---

[25]   Gabriel Zucman, *The Hidden Wealth of Nations* translated by Teresa Lavender Fagan (Chicago: The University of Chicago Press, 2015).

often in an attempt to attract foreign direct investment, may often exhibit similar zero sum qualities to interjurisdictional subsidy and tax competition to attract FDI.

A final issue of controversy relates to monetary unions designed to facilitate the cross-border movement of capital by adopting a common currency that reduces transaction costs and exchange rate risks, the most prominent recent example of which is the adoption in the 1980s by a majority of members of the EU of the euro. In order to maintain a common currency, substantial constraints are required on the ability of member states to adopt their own monetary and fiscal policies and, as the EU experience demonstrates, with members facing very different economic challenges at any given point in time, these constraints come with significant costs and place great weight on the capacity, credibility, and legitimacy of central institutions in framing, adapting, and applying these constraints.[26]

G) COMPETITION POLICY

At the beginning of the Doha Round of multilateral negotiations in 2001, principally on the initiative of the EU, competition policy harmonization was placed on the negotiating agenda, with a view to generating a set of global competition policy norms, perhaps by way of analogy to the TRIPS Agreement negotiated during the Uruguay Round. Proponents of this initiative argued that in an increasingly integrated global economy where business transactions, policies, and practices frequently cross borders, *sui generis* domestic competition policies increasingly risk discordant and dysfunctional outcomes when applied to the same transactions, policies, and practices. In particular, it was argued that harmonized

---

[26] Joseph E. Stiglitz, *The Euro: How a Common Currency Threatens the Future of Europe* (New York: W.W. Norton & Company, 2016).

competition policy approaches were called for with respect to: international cartels and other forms of collusive practices; cross-border mergers and acquisitions potentially affecting competitive conditions in more than one domestic market; and exclusionary or restrictive policies or practices adopted by dominant firms in many markets that require scrutiny as potential abuses of dominance under a common set of criteria.

These proposals generated sharp disagreements amongst member states and were abandoned early in the Doha Round negotiations. Disagreements focused on major divergences in domestic competition law regimes as to both the policy objectives of these regimes and the means chosen to vindicate them in terms of institutional design and decision-making processes.[27]

Many of these divergences with respect to both the ends and means of competition policy seem intractable for the foreseeable future. In the meantime, one should not discount the value of soft law efforts such as those undertaken by the International Competition Network, an international organization of more than 100 domestic competition agencies, to forge at least a loose consensus around best practices on various issues. Nor should one discount the value of mutual cooperation agreements between competition agencies where these are judged to be mutually beneficial.

Beyond these mechanisms, there would seem to be considerable virtue in adhering closely to the principle of nondiscrimination, in particular the National Treatment principle,

---

[27]   Richard Epstein and Michael Greve, eds, *Competition Laws in Conflict: Antitrust Jurisdiction in the Global Economy* (Washington, D.C: AEI Press, 2004); Eleanor Fox and Michael Trebilcock, eds, *The Design of Competition Law Institutions: Global Norms, Local Choices* (Oxford: Oxford University Press, 2013); Damien Gerard and Ioannis Lianos, eds, *Reconciling Efficiency and Equity: A Global Challenge for Competition Policy?* (Cambridge: Cambridge University Press, 2019).

that is a long-standing pillar of the multilateral trade law regime. In particular, with respect to inbound commerce, foreign exporters or investors should be prepared to accept the application of domestic competition policies in countries of destination, provided that they are framed and enforced in a nondiscriminatory fashion with respect to both domestic and foreign firms, even where these laws constrain behaviour that would not be constrained in countries of origin. Conversely, with respect to outbound commerce, firms should not be entitled to complain of lack of access to foreign markets because of barriers to entry that apply in these markets, provided again that these policies are framed and enforced in a nondiscriminatory fashion. However, discordances between domestic competition policies are likely to prove problematic in a residual class of cases that present an all-or-nothing character – for example a proposed mega merger that affects competitive conditions in many domestic markets and is not susceptible to localized remedies. In such cases, there may be virtue in multilateral negotiations around rules of recognition that would identify a lead jurisdiction to undertake primary responsibilities for evaluating such cases, ideally based on the relative impact on consumer welfare in terms of value or volume of sales in the various jurisdictions affected by the transaction or practice in question.[28]

The increasingly significant role of state-owned enterprises (SOEs) as global competitors adds a further dimension of complication to competition policy concerns. Currently, 22 of the world's largest 100 companies and 200 of the largest 2,000 companies are state-owned.[29] While these SOEs historically have served the domestic market, they are engaging increas-

---

[28] Edward Iacobucci and Michael Trebilcock, "Evaluating the Performance of Competition Agencies" in Damien Gerard and Ioannis Lianos, eds, *Reconciling Efficiency and Equity*.

[29] OECD, *State-Owned Enterprises as Global Competitors: A Challenge or an Opportunity?* (Paris: OCED Publishing, 2016).

ingly in cross-border trade. Their increasing prominence as global competitors raises significant concerns for global trade, as interventionist policies that discriminate in favour of them might distort international competition. From a competition law perspective, the presence of SOEs raises several specific concerns. For example, SOEs might pursue non-commercial objectives that might affect their incentives to compete on market-based terms, and some might be exempt from competition law or bankruptcy law in their home jurisdictions, allowing them to engage in anti-competitive practices. In addition, some SOEs enjoy monopoly positions in their domestic markets which might allow them to leverage their monopoly positions into adjacent sectors, for example, by denying access by competitors to essential facilities.[30]

In this context, there is support for a principle of competitive neutrality requiring that SOEs and private businesses compete on a level playing field. Despite this widespread aspiration, however, the application of this principle in practice raises many difficulties. On the conceptual level, it is difficult to determine whether SOEs are cross-subsidizing, pricing at below market levels, or engaging in other anti-competitive conduct. On the political level, competition authorities might not be able to obtain relevant evidentiary information from the foreign state owner of the SOE; even if the wrongdoing can be proved, enforcement against a foreign SOE might also face difficulties; furthermore, even when SOEs are subject to competition law, this might not preclude other advantages and privileges that they are granted; and finally, some jurisdictions with weak rule of law regimes present additional challenges for enforcement.[31]

---

[30]   OECD, *State-Owned Enterprises as Global Competitors: A Challenge or an Opportunity?*

[31]   OECD, *State-Owned Enterprises as Global Competitors: A Challenge or an Opportunity?*

H)   NATIONAL SECURITY

Most international trade and investment regimes provide exceptions permitting restrictions on international trade or investment where justified by national security considerations. These exceptions may permit a country to restrict exports to unfriendly foreign powers of armaments or components thereof, or conversely restrict imports of such products where this may endanger the long-term viability of domestic industries producing these products and whose output may be crucial in the event of international military conflicts or other emergencies in international relations. Foreign direct investments in domestic industries that are important to domestic defence capabilities may often be prohibited or restricted on similar grounds.

The GATT from its inception (Article XXI) has provided for a relatively expansive set of dispensations for national security-related restrictions on international trade. These dispensations attracted very few formal disputes until recent years, reflecting a conventional understanding by members that they were largely self-judging and not subject to detailed scrutiny by the dispute settlement body of the GATT/WTO, but in turn would be sparingly invoked. This conventional understanding has been seriously disrupted in recent years by the invocation by the US Trump Administration of the national security exception in a wide range of cases, including steel and aluminium imports from jurisdictions such as the EU, Canada, and Mexico. Many of such cases are currently the subject of formal dispute settlement proceedings before the WTO, but as noted above, the Trump Administration blocked new appointments to the WTO Appellate Body, seriously undermining the efficacy of the entire dispute resolution regime of the WTO. Other conflicts are looming in high technology or artificial intelligence sectors. For example, the Trump Administration opposed investments by Huawei, a Chinese technology company, in developing 5G networks in the US or other countries, and endorsed restrictions on exports from the US of technology components to Huawei and other Chinese companies on national security grounds: it similarly proposed banning TikTok and WeChat, Chinese-owned social media companies, from the US market.

The Trump Administration also greatly expanded the notion of national security through 2018 legislation called the "Export Controls Act" (ECA). While the US's export control regime previously focused on military-oriented goods and technology, the new ECA expands the concept of national security to also include commercial technology. The new ECA provisions imply that the maintenance and protection of American technological pre-eminence is a matter of national security. As Cindy Whang summarizes in a recent paper,[32] the new ECA differs from its predecessors in three important ways. First, it lacks a termination date. Second, its scope is broadened to include "emerging and foundational technologies", whose content is to be determined by US officials such as the Secretary of Defence, Secretary of Commerce, and Secretary of State. Third, it consolidates national security controls and foreign policy controls into one broad category. In effect, this new ECA proposes the inclusion of emerging technologies into the multilateral export control regime.

This more expansive notion of US national security, which includes the maintenance of technology superiority, is a critical element of the technological issues at the heart of the US–China trade war. There is a significant overlap between the ECA's proposed industries and technologies to be included in its list of emerging technologies and China's list of industries in its "Made in China 2025" Plan to promote emerging technologies. This results in a clash between the industries that the

---

[32] Cindy Whang, "Undermining the Consensus-Building and List-Based Standards in Export Controls: What the US Export Controls Act Means to the Global Export Control Regime" (2019) 22 *JIEL* 579.

US wants to protect and those that China wants to promote in international markets,[33] as I discuss further below in relation to the US–China trade conflict.

I) CULTURAL INDUSTRIES

Many countries have traditionally been concerned that uncon-strained international trade in cultural products, especially films and television programming, is likely to be dominated by a few large jurisdictions that are the home base for major entertainment industries, especially the US, and are likely to find domestic cultural content, with smaller viewer or audi-ence bases, overwhelmed or rendered uneconomic by spillo-ver cultural content from these dominant jurisdictions. Hence, for example, several European countries, most prominently France, have maintained quotas on foreign movies exhibited in domestic cinemas. China has also adopted such a system. Similarly, Canada has historically imposed minimum domes-tic content requirements on most domestic television chan-nels, and imposed foreign ownership restrictions on domestic mass media –television, radio, newspapers, book publishers, and book retailers – to ensure that local voices, perspectives, and concerns receive adequate domestic exposure and thus ensure some significant measure of domestic cultural and political autonomy.

While these concerns often seem legitimate, the rapid evo-lution of modern information and communications technology severely constrains the efficacy of such policies, given the ability of many viewers or listeners to download or stream cul-tural, political, or other content from anywhere in the world on an ever-expanding range of communication conduits. While, of course, such technology also lowers the barriers to entry

---

[33] Cindy Whang, "Undermining the Consensus-Building and List-Based Standards in Export Controls: What the US Export Controls Act Means to the Global Export Control Regime".

for many forms of domestic cultural or political content, such content risks being drowned in the avalanche of information now available to consumers on various platforms, suggesting that rather than trade restrictions, domestic governments in promoting local cultural content and political commentary may need increasingly to resort to subsidy policies to support creative sectors that would otherwise be uneconomic, although subsidy policies in turn raise challenging issues in terms of how they are to be financed and how they are to be administered free of partisan, ideological, or other biases.[34]

J)   HEALTH AND SAFETY STANDARDS[35]

Most trade treaties recognize the right of importing countries to restrict imports where these may pose an unacceptable risk to the health and safety of domestic human, animal, or plant life. For example, Article XX of the GATT permits such measures if necessary for health and safety reasons provided that they do not constitute an arbitrary or unjustifiable form of discrimination or a disguised restriction on trade. The necessity test requires some rough proportionality between the safety benefits of a measure and its adverse effects on trade. In the course of the Uruguay Round, this exception was elaborated in the form of two agreements: the Sanitary and Phytosanitary Measures Agreement (SPS Agreement) and the Technical Barriers to Trade Agreement (TBT Agreement). The first agreement focuses primarily on food safety standards, while the second agreement focuses on all other product standards. In order for domestic food safety regulations to

---

[34]   Lawson A. Hunter, Edward Iacobucci, and Michael J. Trebilcock, "Scrambled Signals: Canadian Content Policies in a World of Technological Abundance" (2010) 301 *C.D. Howe Commentary* 1.

[35]   Michael J. Trebilcock and Joel Trachtman, *Advanced Introduction to International Trade Law*, Chapter 13.

comply with the SPS Agreement, they must either conform to standards set by international standardizing bodies or be based on a scientific risk assessment, as well as meeting general requirements of non-discrimination embodied in the Most Favoured Nation and National Treatment Principles.

Both the GATT health and safety exception in Article XX and the SPS Agreement have generated some significant high-profile international trade disputes. A prominent critique of the SPS Agreement is the centrality that it assigns to either international standards or scientific risk assessments as a justification for trade restrictions on health and safety grounds. In this respect, it is argued that citizens generally differ widely in their subjective assessment of risks and their willingness to bear them, and that these risk preferences are likely to differ from one society to another, whether or not they reflect international standards or prevailing scientific understandings (recognizing, as recent behavioural economics scholarship emphasizes, that subjective assessments of risk often exhibit a wide variety of heuristic biases).[36] Hence it is argued that countries should have wide latitude to adopt trade restrictive health and safety regulations that reflect their own citizens' risk preferences and should not be constrained by either international standards or scientific risk assessments. Ongoing disputes over the regulation of GMOs is a prominent example of these concerns In many respects, they reflect the view of scholars such as Dani Rodrik that globalization, if carried too far, threatens to undermine domestic political sovereignty and democratic decision-making in sovereign states.[37]

This critique has some cogency and again directs us back to the foundational principle of non-discrimination enshrined in the original GATT and embodied in the Most Favoured Nation

---

[36] See e.g., Daniel Kahneman, *Thinking, Fast and Slow* (New York: Anchor, 2011).

[37] Dani Rodrik, *The Globalization Paradox*; Dani Rodrik, *Straight Talk on Trade*.

and National Treatment doctrines. Thus, under these doctrines, an importing state is free to set any domestic health and safety requirements that it chooses – high, low, or anywhere in between – provided only that it applies the same standards to foreign imports as it applies to domestic like products and that it does not play favourites amongst foreigners who meet these standards. As proposed above with respect to the regulation of foreign direct investment, non-discrimination is an enduring and compelling lodestar in regulating international trading and investment relationships by striking a delicate balance between domestic political sovereignty and reasonably free international trade and investment.

However, it should be acknowledged that this balance comes at a cost in terms of international trade. Under the non-discrimination principle – especially the National Treatment principle – foreign firms seeking to export goods to other markets are likely to confront widely diverse health and safety and other product standards that may entail multiple compliance costs and at the limit discourage such firms, especially smaller firms, from entering some of these markets. Hence, pressures will inevitably emerge from export interests to harmonize regulatory standards across markets – a phenomenon perhaps most prominently exemplified in the European Union's Single Market project launched in 1986, but in turn leading to some of the political sentiment in the UK in favour of Brexit.

If one assumes that pre-harmonization regulatory standards in particular countries broadly reflect a given country's societal risk preferences, then any harmonization exercise is likely to entail compromises with these domestic welfare judgements and will often provoke fraught and protracted political tensions across the harmonizing jurisdictions.[38] Delegating

---

[38] Michael Trebilcock and Robert Howse, "Trade Liberalization and Diversity: Reconciling Competitive Politics".

this function to somewhat obscure and opaque international standardizing bodies with limited constituency representation does not necessarily offer an easy way out of these trade-offs, as the SPS Agreement seems to have assumed. This is not to deny that in some cases the argument for harmonization of regulatory standards will be overwhelming – for example, railway gauges, cross-border telephone interconnections, interoperability of various kinds of electronic hardware and software, air traffic control protocols and so on, where discordant regulations achieve no compelling social purpose and often entail serious social costs. However, in other domains sensitivity to differences in domestic risk preferences is likely to be much more salient.

There is no easy resolution of these trade-offs, although for my part I would prefer not to stray too far from the non-discrimination principle, which should not be elided with an unconstrained trade liberalization principle.

K)   ENVIRONMENTAL STANDARDS[39]

In some respects, the issue of compliance with environmental standards in trade across national borders raises similar issues to compliance with health and safety regulations in different jurisdictions. Most trade treaties contain provisions that permit importing countries to restrict imports that are non-compliant with domestic environmental regulations provided that these are applied in a non-discriminatory fashion to imports relative to domestically produced like products.

More controversy surrounds attempts by importing countries to enforce environmental regulations against harms arising outside their territorial jurisdiction. For example, in the early to mid-1990s the GATT/WTO dispute settlement

---

[39]   Michael J. Trebilcock and Joel Trachtman, *Advanced Introduction to International Trade Law*, Chapter 14.

body held that US fisheries regulations that required their own fishing fleet to adopt fishing methods that minimized harm to dolphins in the course of fishing for tuna could not be extended to imports of tuna caught by noncompliant fishing fleets outside US territorial waters. Similarly, in early decisions the WTO dispute settlement body held that US fisheries regulations that required special turtle excluder devices in nets when fishing for shrimp could not be extended to imports of shrimp caught by other methods beyond its territorial waters. In further dispute resolution proceedings, a modified version of the US regulations was upheld, in that it provided some flexibility for foreign fishing fleets and their governments to demonstrate that the fishing techniques adopted were of comparable effectiveness to those required of US fishing fleets. In this case, the turtles in question were listed as an endangered species under the Convention on International Trade in Endangered Species. The Appellate Body clarified that in this context the fact that the environmental harm might occur beyond the territorial jurisdiction of the country seeking to enforce its domestic environmental regulations was not a bar to enforcement. In a later case involving an EU prohibition on the sale or importation of products made from seal skins, the rationale for which was objections to inhumane seal harvesting methods adopted in Canada, in particular, the WTO dispute settlement body recognized that these regulations could be justified under the public morals exception in the GATT (Article XX), provided that these were applied in a non-discriminatory fashion, which an exception for Inuit seal harvesting in Greenland was held to violate.

A more controversial and debatable argument is sometimes made for more expansive derogations from trade commitments on environmental grounds to the effect that exporting countries with laxer domestic environmental regulations than importing countries are engaged in an unacceptable form of "social dumping" that justifies importing countries imposing duties or other trade restrictions, by way of analogy with economic forms of dumping. However, this argument is unpersuasive in the absence of cross-border environmental externalities of some kind that other countries who bear these externalities might well be justified in sanctioning, including by trade sanctions. There are many reasons why domestic environmental regulations that address purely domestic environmental harms may vary significantly from one country to another, including geographic and climatic factors, population densities, structure of economic activities, and differences in preferences for trade-offs between environmental harms and economic well-being.

Even in cases where economic activities in one country generate environmental externalities for other countries (as in the Tuna–Dolphin and Shrimp–Turtles cases noted above), the appropriate response, including possible trade sanctions, is likely to be controversial. Overwhelmingly the most important contemporary exemplar of these issues is climate change policy. Greenhouse gas emissions have the same impact on global warming irrespective of their source and hence generate a global environmental externality that all countries bear, in principle requiring a coordinated global response, which to date has proven elusive, although the Paris Climate Change Accord entered into by more than 180 countries in 2015 (from which the US Trump Administration subsequently withdrew) suggests at least the potential for coordinated global action.

However, in the meantime, many countries have chosen to undertake, or are contemplating undertaking, unilateral action to reduce greenhouse gas emissions in their own jurisdiction through, for example, carbon taxes or cap and trade regimes. Such regimes, if adopted unilaterally, inevitably raise the question of the treatment of imported products that do not meet the requirements of these regimes. In the worst-case scenario such regimes are likely to induce the movement of investment, jobs, and greenhouse gas emissions to other jurisdictions that have adopted much laxer regulation of greenhouse gas emissions. At the limit, this would be an exercise in environmental futility as well as a political and economic suicide mission for any government contemplating the unilateral adoption of more stringent regimes. Thus, proponents of such regimes typically contemplate that they will be complemented by so-called carbon tariffs at the border that impose on imported products the same environmental mitigation burdens that domestic regulations impose on domestic producers of like products.

The legality of such measures has not yet been authoritatively ruled on by the dispute settlement body of the WTO, but may well be justified under the health and safety and environmental exceptions in the GATT, noted above, provided that they are applied in a non-discriminatory fashion.[40] Applying the non-discrimination principle in this context poses its own set of challenges. Some countries (especially developing countries) will argue that historically they have been much more minor contributors to the stock of greenhouse gases in the atmosphere than many importing developed countries, and should not bear the same burden of abatement, or that they are at an earlier stage of economic development than importing countries and face different policy trade-offs than the latter. Yet other countries will argue that they have adopted a constellation of *sui generis* environmental policies appropriate to their climate, geography, and economic structure that are comparable in effectiveness to the policies adopted by importing countries and should be exempt from any border carbon tariffs. These are enormously complex and contentious issues, and may well tax both the institutional competence and the legitimacy of the WTO dispute settlement body (already facing serious challenges on this score). This returns us to the centrality of coordinated global responses, notwithstanding

---

[40] Michael J. Trebilcock and Joel Trachtman, *Advanced Introduction to International Trade Law*, pp.194–197.

the formidable collective action and free rider problems that such responses must inevitably confront.

L)   LABOUR STANDARDS[41]

A yet further and equally intense set of controversies surround divergent domestic labour standards and regulations in cross-border trade. Here the cleavages between developed and developing countries are sharp and reciprocal. On the one hand, developed countries often argue that their domestic industries should not have to compete with imports from countries with much lower cost unskilled labour, at least where these countries do not adhere to basic labour standards that typically obtain in developed countries – for example the core labour standards promulgated by the International Labour Organization (ILO) in its 1998 Declaration on Fundamental Principles and Rights at Work, that is, freedom of association; the elimination of forced labour; the elimination of child labour; and the elimination of discrimination in employment. On the other hand, developing countries often argue that they should not have to compete with imported goods and services produced by highly skilled workers in developed countries, and, invoking infant industry rationales, argue that they should be able to protect domestic providers of goods and services, at least in the early stages of the development of these sectors, from import competition from providers in developed countries. These offsetting arguments, if taken to an extreme, would constitute a massive barrier to most forms of trade between developed and developing countries.

To take the developed country argument first, one of the major sources of comparative advantage for many developing countries is low cost, relatively unskilled labour, at least once

---

[41] Michael J. Trebilcock and Joel Trachtman, *Advanced Introduction to International Trade Law*, Chapter 15.

one has accounted for differences in the productivity of labour across countries. Moreover, consumers in developed countries benefit from lower cost imports equivalent to an increase in their real income and their increased purchasing power should be treated as an equivalent to an increase in their real incomes, which will typically exceed income losses by firms and their workers in import-impacted sectors. Indeed, lower-income consumers spend a higher proportion of their incomes than higher-income consumers and spend a higher proportion of their incomes on imported products.[42] Thus, crude nationalist or nativist arguments for "keeping jobs at home" defy the central logic of the gains from the division of labour and specialization that lie at the core of international trade theory. However, one cannot dismiss out of hand the argument that certain basic labour standards should be viewed as akin to universal human rights that for intrinsic reasons require a respect for basic human dignity and should be observed across the world. The ILO's core labour standards may be justified in these non-consequentialist terms. However, two major sets of issues must then be confronted.

First, these core labour standards are not self-defining. For example, amongst developed countries the scope of collective bargaining varies widely from one country to another in terms of some essential service sectors being excluded from the right to strike; whether union membership and dues are mandatory; whether replacement workers can be hired in the event of a strike. What constitutes objectionable forms of child labour is also open to debate, given that even in developed countries to the present day children often help out with chores on family farms or in small family businesses, or in times not so distant ran neighbourhood newspaper routes; forced labour may range all the way from outright slavery to

---

[42] Kimberly Clausing, *Open: The Progressive Case for Free Trade, Immigration, and Global Capital* (Cambridge, MA: Harvard University Press, 2019).

human trafficking to bonded peasant labour, to noncompete clauses in employment contracts. Discrimination in the workplace on the basis of race, religion, or gender may often be explicit and clearly invidious, but disparate-impact forms of discrimination are often less obvious and more contentious.

Second, even if generalized agreement across countries can be achieved on the content of core labour standards, issues must then be confronted as to how they should be enforced. Trade sanctions against imports from infringing countries are one option, although core labour standard violations often occur in non-traded sectors – this is especially the case with child labour. As well, it is important to assess the impact of trade sanctions on all parties, including workers in foreign countries that are not implicated in these violations but are adversely affected by trade sanctions. Moreover, concerns legitimately arise as to whether the potential for trade sanctions against imports are likely to be opportunistically abused by domestic producer interests in importing countries for purely protectionist reasons, such as insisting on minimum wage levels for foreign workers comparable to those prevailing in importing countries (as in the rules governing auto trade under the renegotiated NAFTA (USMCA) which require that a high percentage of value-added in auto manufacturing be provided by workers earning at least $16 per hour).

Alternatives to trade sanctions should also be considered. For example, trade preferences granted by developed countries to developing countries pursuant to Special and Differential Treatment for developing countries might be conditioned on adherence to well-specified core labour standards. Foreign aid to such countries might similarly be conditioned. Or alternatively, reliance could be placed mostly on soft law – for example the naming and shaming mechanisms employed by the ILO for countries found to be noncompliant with their ILO commitments. Alternatively, again, one could rely mostly on private initiatives such as corporate social responsibility codes or voluntary labelling systems designed to inform consumers in importing countries of compliance by foreign producers with core labour standards, although private codes of conduct and labelling systems often present consumers in importing countries with major informational challenges in determining what standards they adopt and how well they are monitored and enforced – especially in the case of products that are the final output of complex global supply chains – as well as the risk of effective consumer responses being undermined by collective action/free rider problems.

It is difficult to be dogmatic about the ideal or preferable response to trading relationships with countries alleged to be in violation of core labour standards, and the relative efficacy of responses is likely to depend heavily on context. However, unlike some prominent globalization proponents,[43] I do not dismiss out of hand the appropriateness of trade sanctions in some contexts. While they do not fall within an explicit exception of the GATT, they may well be justified under the public morals exception in Article XX, by way of analogy to trade sanctions that have been upheld in the case of inhumane seal harvesting methods (discussed above), provided that they meet the prefatory conditions in Article XX, that is, that the measures in question are not an arbitrary or unjustifiable form of discrimination or a disguised restriction on trade. To take an extreme case, should we trade with countries with respect to products made literally by slave labour, as occurred widely in the 16th, 17th, and 18th centuries (as discussed above)? Surely not, if basic universal human rights have any content at all. While literal slavery has been abolished in most parts of the world (although human trafficking still remains a significant phenomenon), some contemporary employment relationships share significant similarities with slavery (e.g., China's use of forced Xighur labour) and may warrant formal

---

[43] Martin Wolf, *Why Globalization Works* (New Haven: Yale University Press, 2004); Jagdish Bhagwati, *In Defense of Globalization* (New York: Oxford University Press, 2004).

disopprobrium, in some of the more egregious cases through trade and other economic sanctions.

More generally, it is easy to exaggerate the impact of imports from low-wage countries on economic welfare in developed countries. For example, one might usefully compare GDP at purchasing power parity in international dollars for 2017 for the US, Mexico, China, and India (three developing countries that have recently attracted the ire of the US Trump Administration):

United States: 59,927
Mexico: 18,655
China: 16,842
India: 7,166

In the case of all three developing countries, per capita incomes are a small fraction of those prevailing in the US, and in absolute terms the differentials may actually have increased since 1990, while hundreds of millions of residents of China and other developing countries have been lifted out of poverty over this period. This is not to deny that importation of products from low-wage countries has had a significant impact on the manufacturing sector in the US and the workers employed in that sector. Several million jobs have been lost in this sector over the past decade or so, although at the same time manufacturing output has actually increased. Most estimates suggest that at most 20 to 25 percent of these jobs have been lost to trade, while the rest have been lost to technology, that is, the substitution of capital for labour, while acknowledging that disentangling the effects of trade and technology on domestic labour markets is not straightforward – sometimes they are substitutes, in other cases complements. Whatever the causes of job loss, active labour market policies and an extensive social safety net are critically important elements in an effective policy response to adverse labour market impacts that reflect long-term structural shifts in the economy. A comparative review of such policies suggests that some countries have done much better than others in mitigating the transition costs associated with such structural changes.[44] In this respect, the US does not compare well with a number of European countries who have devoted many more resources to these policies than the relatively paltry amount that the US devotes to them.

While the safeguard regime enshrined in the GATT from its inception (Article XIX) and now the Uruguay Round Safeguards Agreement, permit temporary import restrictions to moderate the impact of import surges due to unforeseen circumstances, this regime has played a minor role in moderating adverse labour market impacts: first, the Appellate Body has interpreted its requirements in such a restrictive and confusing fashion that very few measures have survived scrutiny by it; second, where safeguard measures have been imposed, the evidence suggests that they cost consumers in aggregate several multiples of the value of each job saved and often entail even greater job losses in downstream industries that use inputs from the domestic industry protected by the safeguards; and finally, safeguard measures by definition only mitigate job losses from trade and not technology, implying that broader gauge labour market and social safety net policies are likely to be both more effective and more equitable in the long run.[45]

A related set of concerns relates to the impact of international trade on globalization more generally in rising levels

---

[44]   Michael Trebilcock and Sally Wong, "Trade, Technology and Transitions: Trampolines or Safety Nets for Displaced Workers?" (2018) 21 *Journal of International Economic Law* 509; Martin Sandbu, *The Economics of Belonging: A Radical Plan to Win Back the Left Behind and Achieve Prosperity for All* (Princeton University Press, 2020).

[45]   David H. Autor, "Trade and Labour Markets: Lessons from China's Rise" (2018) *IZA World of Labor* 431.

of inequality in many developed (and some developing) countries in recent decades – exhaustively documented by Thomas Piketty and other scholars.[46] While properly a matter of serious concern, it is not clear that international trade has been a major contribution to these trends, as opposed to skill-biased technological change, or even increased concentration in many sectors of developed countries' economies.[47] While increased capital mobility has no doubt caused significant job losses, and put downward pressure on wages in remaining jobs in some sectors, and also compromised the ability of governments to maintain effective tax policies, these effects are likely dominated by the effects of technological change. Moreover, while within-country levels of inequality have been rising in many cases, between-country levels of inequality, at least on a population-weighted basis, have been declining, reflecting rising per capita incomes in many developing countries.[48]

As to the reciprocal objection by many developing countries to unconstrained trade with developed countries, particularly with respect to products and services that are intensive in highly skilled labour, this is merely a restatement of the infant industry argument for protectionism in the early stages

---

[46] Thomas Piketty, *Capitalism in the 21st Century* translated by Arthur Goldhammer (Cambridge, MA: The Belknap Press of Harvard University Press, 2014); Thomas Piketty, *Capitalism and Ideology* translated by Arthur Goldhammer (Cambridge, MA: Harvard University Press, 2020).

[47] Elhanan Helpman, *Globalization and Inequality* (Cambridge, MA: Harvard University Press, 2018); Thomas Philippon, *The Great Reversal: How America Gave Up on Free Markets* (Cambridge, MA: The Belknap Press of Harvard University Press, 2019).

[48] Branko Milanovic, *Global Inequality: A New Approach for the Age of Globalization* (Cambridge, MA: The Belknap Press of Harvard University Press, 2016); Francois Bourguignon, *The Globalization of Inequality* translated by Thomas Scott-Railton (Princeton: Princeton University Press, 2015); Richard Baldwin, *The Great Convergence*; Steven Radelet, *The Great Surge*.

of a country's economic development that I reviewed in an earlier section of this book, and is as strong or weak as one considers the general arguments for infant industry protection. However, since the time that special dispensations were granted to developing countries on both the import side in the mid-1950s and on the export side in the mid-1960s, endogenous growth theory, associated most prominently with the 2018 Nobel Laureate in economics, Paul Romer, has emphasized the importance of rapid diffusion and adaptation of ideas and technological innovations, often originating in developed countries, in promoting economic growth in developing countries in agricultural, manufacturing, and service sectors, as well as in the provision of health care and education.[49] This factor must be included in the already mixed balance sheet surrounding infant industry protection policies.

M)   HUMAN RIGHTS[50]

The relationship between international trade law and policies, on the one hand, and international or universal human rights norms, on the other, raises similar issues, in some respects, to those relating to divergences in labour market standards.

At the time of the formation of the GATT in 1947, international universal human rights laws and norms were not well developed and they are not accorded any explicit recognition in the GATT, beyond the potential application of the undefined public morals exception in the GATT (Article XX). Notwithstanding the absence of any acknowledged linkage between trade policy and human rights, trade sanctions over the intervening years have been unilaterally invoked against

---

[49]   See also Diego Comin and Bart Hobijn, "An Exploration of Technology Diffusion" (2010) 100 *American Economic Review* 2031.

[50]   Michael J. Trebilcock and Joel Trachtman, *Advanced Introduction to International Trade Law*, Chapter 15.

countries judged to be in serious violation of international human rights norms, such as freedom from genocide, torture, arbitrary arrest or detention without trial, or systematic persecution of racial or religious minorities. Perhaps the most prominent example is the set of economic sanctions invoked by a number of countries in the mid to late 1980s against the apartheid regime in South Africa (a direct extension of the segregationist policies originally established by British and Dutch colonizing powers in South Africa), and at the request of South African leaders of the anti-apartheid movement. The sanctions typically entailed extensive restrictions on imports from South Africa and restrictions on foreign direct investment in Africa. While there is room for the debate about the relative impact of these sanctions in inducing the end of the apartheid regime, as with trade sanctions directed at violations of core labour standards in exporting countries the efficacy of trade sanctions directed at human rights violations needs to be compared with the alternatives available – for example, the withdrawal of foreign aid where applicable; diplomatic protests or termination of diplomatic relationships at one end of the spectrum, to military invasion at the other. Again, one cannot be dogmatic about the relative efficacy of alternative responses by countries to egregious human rights abuses by other countries, which is likely to depend on context and relationships, and in some cases may argue for a coordinated international response through UN organs such as the Security Council (which it must be acknowledged suffers from its own set of dysfunctions), or naming and shaming through UN Human Rights committees. For example, economic sanctions against the Saddam Hussein regime in Iraq and the current Iranian regime may have been less successful than economic sanctions against the apartheid regime in South Africa. Economic sanctions against China for its repression of its Muslim minorities may have little effect. Military invasions also have a mixed record, as for example with the US invasions of Vietnam, Iraq, and Afghanistan. However, as with

core labour standards, one cannot rule out of hand the invocation of trade sanctions against countries seriously delinquent
in their observance of basic human rights norms.

N) DIGITAL TRADE, PRIVACY AND CYBER SECURITY

The rise of digital trade and modern computing technologies
has greatly facilitated international trade, as is evident in
the growing importance of digital communications, digital
commerce, digitally capable products, digitally delivered
and enabled services, and digitally delivered work, amongst
others.[51] The increased capacity to enter into transactions,
deliver goods and services, and share large quantities of data
over the internet has the potential to increase human wealth
and well-being, but at the same time raises difficult legal and
ethical issues for international trade law, particularly in the
areas of privacy and cyber security.[52]

For individual consumers, privacy is a significant concern
raised by new digital technologies. Personal information has
become an important new currency in the global market, and
to a certain extent personal data has been commodified.[53]
Examples of technological applications that realize the com-
modification and commercialization of personal information
include plans to sell the VeriChip, an implantable chip that
contains the human subject's medical history and information;
plans to commercialize the wOzNet, a wearable identification
device; and others.[54] Another example is the "Internet of

---

[51] Michael Trebilcock and Joel Trachtman, *Advanced
Introduction to International Trade Law*, Chapter 17.
[52] Michael J. Trebilcock and Joel Trachtman, *Advanced
Introduction to International Trade Law*, Chapter 17.
[53] Paul M. Schwartz, "Property, Privacy and Personal Data"
(2004) 117 *Harvard Law Review* 2056.
[54] Paul M. Schwartz, "Property, Privacy and Personal Data".

Things", which is at its core characterized by the combination of physical and digital components to create a new network of digitally enabled products.[55] Examples include "smart" devices ranging from cellphones to washing machines to wearable devices that are connected to the internet. One estimate suggests that there are approximately 21 billion "things" connected to the internet at this moment, most of which are consumer devices.[56] This new technological architecture allows for the collection of massive amounts of individual information, and sometimes for individuals to be tracked and followed even without their knowledge.[57]

Another concern to states and individuals alike is the threat that digital trade poses to cybersecurity, which grows as digital connectivity increases. Potential cybersecurity threats include the theft of intellectual property, manipulation of online information (including interfering in domestic electoral processes), hacking, cyber espionage, and cyber attacks on a country's critical infrastructure. Recently under the Trump Administration, the US's National Security Telecommunications Advisory Council characterized cybersecurity as an aspect of national security and excluded Huawei,TikTok and WeChat from the US market ostensibly on these grounds. Beyond the United States, at least 50 per cent of countries around the world have adopted similar positions and implemented new policies and regulations in response to rising cybersecurity threats.[58]

---

[55] Felix Wortmann, Kristina Fluchter, "Internet of Things: Technology and Value Added" (2015) 57 *Business & Information Systems Engineering* 221.

[56] Eric Knorr, "The Internet of Things in 2020: More Vital than Ever" (May 11, 2020) *Network World* (blog), online: <https://www.networkworld.com/article/3542891/the-internet-of-things-in-2020-more-vital-than-ever.html>.

[57] Rolf H. Weber, "Internet of Things – New Security and Privacy Challenges" (2010) 26 *Computer Law & Security Review* 23.

[58] Joshua P. Meltzer, "Cybersecurity, Digital Trade, and Data Flows: Re-thinking a Role for International Trade Rules", *Brookings*

Beginning in 1995, the WTO began to regulate cross-border data flows through the GATS, which contains annexes on financial services, computer services, and telecommunications, complemented by the Agreement on Trade-Related Aspects of Intellectual Property Rights (TRIPS), which protects intellectual property related to information technology, the Information Technology Agreement (ITA) in 1996, which eliminated duties for trade in computing and information technology equipment, and the adoption of the Global Work Programme on Electronic Commerce in 1998. However, it remains an open question whether these initiatives have the potential to meet the challenges of digital trade.

The most directly relevant provisions in WTO law that relate to digital trade are found in the GATS. This agreement contains general obligations such as the Most Favoured Nation commitment, which applies to all services, and each member's specific scheduled commitments, which include National Treatment and market access obligations. Thus, if a country implements a measure that restricts data flows and digital trade, it could violate its GATS obligations, but these violations are subject to both general exceptions found in GATS Article XIV and the security exception found in GATS Article XIV bis. One of the most relevant exceptions for cybersecurity is the national security exception of Article XIV bis (b)(iii) which states that nothing in the GATS shall be construed "to prevent any Member from taking any action which it considers necessary for the protection if its essential security interests […] taken in time of war or other emergency in international relations." This exception could theoretically justify data restrictive measures that are claimed to be necessary to protect "essential security interests" in the context of an international relations emergency, such as threats of cyber attacks or cyber espionage. However, due to the paucity of

WTO jurisprudence in this area and the inherent ambiguity in the meaning of key terms of the provision like "essential security interests" and "war or other emergency in international relations," this provision leaves open the question of what kinds of threats in the digital realm, if any, constitute an emergency that justifies data restrictive measures.[59]

Beyond the national security exception, members could also look to general exceptions under the GATS. For example, under Article XIV(c)(ii), the GATS allows members to adopt domestic policies that restrict data flows for the protection of individual privacy and confidentiality.[60] In addition, Article XIV(c)(i), which provides an exception for the prevention of deceptive and fraudulent practices, and Article XIV(c)(iii), which provides an exception for health and safety measures, could be interpreted to cover cybersecurity policies, even though cybersecurity is not explicitly mentioned. Furthermore, Article XIV (a) could apply if a data restrictive cybersecurity measure is necessary to maintain public order.[61] However, to justify any of these general exceptions requires meeting the necessity test, which weighs several factors such as the contribution that the measure makes to the enforcement of the policy objective, compared to its restrictive effect on international trade in services. Once necessity is provisionally demonstrated, the opposing party can rebut this necessity by

---

[59] Martina Francesca Ferracane, "GATS Security Exception: What if It Were to Be Invoked to Justify Restrictions on Data Flows?" (February 2019) *APEC Currents* (blog), online: <https://www.apec.org.au/apec-currents-2019-feb-gats>.

[60] Andrew D. Mitchell and Neha Mishra, "Regulating Cross-Border Data Flows in a Data-Driven World: How WTO Law Can Contribute" (2019) 22 *Journal of International Economic Law* 389.

[61] Andrew D. Mitchell and Neha Mishra, "Regulating Cross-Border Data Flows in a Data-Driven World: How WTO Law Can Contribute".

demonstrating that a less trade restrictive measure is reasonably available.[62]

More importantly, the GATS was concluded in a pre-internet era, and its applicability to digital trade today is limited, as many current technologies were not envisaged at the time of its negotiation. For example, it is unclear whether new digital services that did not exist at the time of negotiation, like search engines and cloud computing, are covered by members' GATS commitment schedules. Furthermore, classification issues in the digital economy raise new challenges for the GATS. For example, because of the cross-cutting and integrated nature of digital services, many businesses bundle various types of services to provide an online service, making it difficult to determine whether the service in question is covered by a member's scheduled GATS commitments.[63] In addition, some forms of cross-border data flows such as those related to the "internet of things" contain both services *and* goods components, each of which are governed by distinct WTO disciplines. However, it is often difficult to separate the services-related and goods-related aspects of a digital product for the purposes of determining which trade disciplines apply.[64] Another problem that arises is the difficulty in determining "likeness" when applying the Most Favoured Nation commitment and National Treatment obligations, for example whether electronically delivered services and services deliv-

---

[62] Svetlana Yakovleva and Kristina Irion, "Pitching Trade against Privacy: Reconciling EU Governance of Personal Data Flows with External Trade" (2020) 0 *International Data Privacy Law* 1.

[63] Joshua P. Metlzer, "Governing Digital Trade" (2019) 18 *World Trade Review* 23.

[64] Andrew D. Mitchell and Neha Mishra, "Regulating Cross-Border Data Flows in a Data-Driven World: How WTO Law Can Contribute".

ered by more traditional methods should be considered "like services".[65]

In response, many recently concluded PTAs have followed the "GATS-plus" criteria by going beyond the original scope of the GATS. These agreements endorse digital trade generally but adopt new provisions that regulate data flows in a way that balances the interests of privacy and trade liberalization.[66] Some newer PTAs contain chapters on digital trade that address issues in global data flows, for example, through data localization, which requires entities processing data of a given country's citizens to store that data domestically on servers within the country's borders.[67] The US has spearheaded the negotiation of e-commerce chapters in PTAs since 2000. Other countries have followed and now these chapters are a common feature of PTAs, as reflected in the recent negotiation of the Regional Comprehensive Economic Partnership (RCEP) and renegotiation of NAFTA. However, as a result of the proliferation of electronic commerce chapters in PTAs, the WTO's multilateral trade law have lagged behind PTAs, and sometimes the two may even conflict.[68]

Given these concerns, scholars have largely agreed on the need for a set of updated multilateral trade rules suited to the

---

[65] Sacha Wunsch-Vincent, "Trade Rules for the Digital Age" in Marion Panizzon, Nicole Pohl, and Pierre Sauvé, eds, *GATS and the Regulation of International Trade in Services* (Cambridge: Cambridge University Press, 2008).

[66] Svetlana Yakovleva and Kristina Irion, "Pitching Trade against Privacy: Reconciling EU Governance of Personal Data Flows with External Trade".

[67] Ethan Loufield and Shweta Vashisht, "Data Globalization vs. Data Localization" (February 6, 2020) *Center for Financial Inclusion* (blog), online: <https://www.centerforfinancialinclusion.org/data-globalization-vs-data-localization>.

[68] Andrew D. Mitchell and Neha Mishra, "Data at the Docks: Modernizing International Trade Law for the Digital Economy" (2018) 20 *Vanderbilt Journal of Entertainment & Technology Law* 1073.

digital age. First, as many scholars have suggested, the benefits of cross-border data flow needs to be balanced with concerns about security and privacy. Thus, future trade rules need to offer protections of personal data, but also avoid excessive data localization requirements which risk new forms of digital protectionism.[69] How to strike this balance, however, remains a difficult question, as evident in recent disputes over digital trade restrictions between the US and China. In response to China's data security and privacy measures including restrictions on foreign-invested cloud computing services, web filtering and blocking technologies (such as the national firewall), and data localization requirements, the Office of the US Trade Representative released a report in 2017 labelling China's policies as disruptive digital trade barriers and instances of digital protectionism, which impose significant costs on suppliers and users of web-based services and products and prejudice foreign internet service suppliers.[70]

Second, some scholars suggest that there should be a set of standard duties or taxes for digital goods and services, set at a level to ensure that duties do not inhibit trade growth and liberalization. The standardization of duties would provide greater certainty for digital trade. These kinds of duties are already included in many PTAs, but multilateral rules would provide a more level playing field.[71] However, reaching a consensus on the level of duties has also proven to be a contentious issue, as reflected in the recent dispute between the US

---

[69]   Vinay Mendonca, "Here's How We Reboot Digital Trade for the 21st Century" (July 25, 2019) *World Economic Forum* (blog), online: <https://www.weforum.org/agenda/2019/07/heres-how-we-reboot-digital-trade-for-the-21st-century>.

[70]   Office of the United States Trade Representative, "Key Barriers to Digital Trade", *Office of the United States Trade Representative* (March 2017), online: <https://ustr.gov/about-us/policy-offices/press-office/fact-sheets/2017/march/key-barriers-digital-trade>.

[71]   Vinay Mendonca, "Here's How We Reboot Digital Trade for the 21st Century".

and EU over digital taxes. When EU countries released their digital tax plans, the US Trump Administration responded aggressively, announcing that it would retaliate with tariffs. While the EU argued that corporate tax rules need to reflect digital realities and new ways that businesses profit from digital services in countries without being physically present, the US administration was concerned that the taxes would hit American tech giants hardest. Despite the benefits of certainty of a standardized digital tax regime, current disagreements raise concerns over the emergence of a new digital dimension to global trade conflicts.[72]

O)   MIGRANTS ACTUAL AND VIRTUAL

As noted in an earlier section, cross-border movement of people is subject to much less international coordination through treaties than cross-border movement of goods, services or capital, with the notable exception of the EU which guarantees the free movement of citizens and permanent residents across its member states. Some regional trade agreements such as NAFTA (now USMCA) and the Australia–New Zealand free trade agreement provide for cross-border movement of temporary workers of various categories, especially professional or technical workers. Multilaterally, only the 1951 Geneva Convention on Refugees imposes on its signatories obligations to evaluate in-land refugee claimants against generalized criteria, in particular well-founded apprehensions of persecution on account of race, religion, or political beliefs in claimants' home countries. It does not address the challenge of burden sharing among recipient countries – a problem thrown into sharp relief in 2015 with a major influx of refu-

---

[72]   Alan Rappeport and Jim Tankersley, "Digital Tax Fight Emerges as Global Economic Threat", *The New York Times* (February 22, 2020), online: <https://www.nytimes.com/2020/02/22/us/politics/digital-tax-economy-europe-united-states.html>.

gees and destitute migrants from Syria and North Africa into the southern countries of the EU.

As to the optimal set of immigration policies for recipient countries, these have raised complex and highly contentious issues in many developed countries in recent years. A core challenge is that migrants fall into many different categories that may legitimately justify different policies.[73] At one end of the spectrum are highly skilled professional or technical workers who are often in much demand in increasingly knowledge and technology intensive economies, and are likely to create more jobs than they displace and contribute more in tax revenues than their demands on social programmes. Immigrants or their children are heavily over-represented in the US as founders or co-founders of high tech start-ups, Fortune 500 companies, and Nobel Laureates.[74] Some countries, such as Canada, Australia, and New Zealand, have adopted point systems, rather than formal quotas (as in the US), to evaluate the admissibility of such migrants. Next along the spectrum are foreign students who in the course of their advanced studies in host countries may often acquire skills, knowledge, and language abilities that make them highly valuable potential employees or entrepreneurs in host countries, and may warrant relatively expansive admissibility criteria. Further along the spectrum are less skilled or unskilled workers who in some cases may fill permanent gaps in a receiving country's labour force – for example, personal care workers or nannies – and it seems appropriate that after some relatively short period of continuous employment they should qualify for permanent resident status: other semi-skilled or unskilled workers may meet seasonal labour demands, such as in the agricultural sector, and may warrant short-term admission. Further along the spectrum are refugees or destitute migrants

---

[73]   Michael J. Trebilcock, *Dealing with Losers*, Chapter 7.
[74]   Kimberly Clausing, *Open*.

who unilaterally arrive in or at the borders of recipient countries and raise claims requiring evaluation on humanitarian grounds, recognizing that no single recipient country has unlimited capacity to admit all such migrants – a fraught issue currently in the US, the EU, and other countries. Somewhere else on the spectrum are family sponsored migrants, where citizens or permanent residents may wish to sponsor close family members, for example spouses or minor children who are residents of other countries, whether or not they meet the employability criteria applied to other classes of migrants, arguably justifying imposing on sponsors some form of mandatory bonding or insurance coverage against drawings by sponsored family members on social benefit programmes for some period of time after arrival.

With respect to both the highly skilled and foreign student categories of potential migrants, it is often argued that expansive admissibility criteria in developed countries represent a form of "cherry picking" that risks a brain drain from many developing countries where highly skilled workers in many sectors, including their health and education sectors, are often in desperately short supply. This concern has some cogency, although it is difficult to deny on human rights grounds the right of individuals, if they so choose, to exit their countries of residence and move to other countries willing to receive them. Moreover, remittances from emigrants to their home countries have recently exceeded $500 billion a year – about three times the amount of official foreign aid assistance. As well, the mere option of emigrating often provides an incentive for students (and their parents) in developing countries to invest in higher education even if in many cases this option is not exercised.

Recently, in a provocative book, *The Globotics Revolution*, Richard Baldwin argues that the next and imminent globalization frontier will involve remote or virtual highly skilled immigrants, often based in low-wage developing countries, providing a wide range of services remotely to firms and consumers in developed countries through the rapidly expanding capabilities of robotics and other forms of artificial intelligence, which may threaten many white-collar jobs in these countries, in contrast to the expansion of trade with low-wage developed countries in manufactured goods, which has mostly threatened blue-collar jobs in developed countries. This phenomenon is likely to evolve with or without formal commitments by developed countries to open up their service sectors to international competition under GATS, and while developed countries may attempt to regulate this form of cross-border service provision by requiring domestic service consumers to utilize domestic service providers, the electronic transmission of these services is likely to make effective regulation extremely challenging (as is already evident by the extensive provision of back office services by providers in India and elsewhere).

P)   FOOD SECURITY[75]

For most governments in both developed and developing countries, one of their core functions is to ensure access to affordable food and ensure that their citizens do not die of hunger or risk serious health deficits as a result of malnutrition. While the incidence of hunger and malnutrition has declined sharply in most countries over the post-war decades, it continues to be a pressing problem in some countries and in times of conflict or turbulence in international relations at least a prospective problem in many more, often leading to arguments for a high degree of self-sufficiency in food production. To this end, it is then argued that trade restrictions on imported foodstuffs are justifiable in order to protect and promote local sources of supply. To some extent, reflecting these arguments, in the post-war period the agricultural sector

---

[75]   Michael J. Trebilcock and Joel Trachtman, *Advanced Introduction to International Trade Law*, Chapter 9.

in many developed countries has been subject to much higher levels of trade protectionism than other sectors, as well as in many cases export and domestic subsidies. In some cases, tariffs on imported food products run into several hundred percent.[76]

It is far from clear that these policies are justified by the rationales typically offered for them. First, they are often extremely costly to developing countries who are denied export opportunities for agricultural products in which they have a comparative advantage. Second, it is not clear in many cases that domestic self-sufficiency in food production is the optimal strategy for minimizing risks to the food supply chain. Indeed, if floods, droughts, or pestilence predominantly strike a country's own agricultural sector, self-sufficiency may exacerbate these risks. A striking example that illustrates this point is the case of Singapore, a small city-state that produces almost none of its own food but is rated as one of the top countries in the world in terms of food security, largely by prudent diversification of foreign sources of supply.[77] While the GATT (Article XI) from its inception has permitted countries facing a shortage of food or other essential products to restrict exports on a temporary basis, recognizing understandably that a country's government's first obligation is to ensure that its citizens do not starve, there are strong arguments for restraint in invoking this exception, as exemplified by the responses of some governments to a dramatic run-up in world grain prices in 2007–2008. These responses often entailed imposing

---

[76] Michael Trebilcock and Kristen Pue, "The Puzzle of Agricultural Exceptionalism in International Trade Policy" (2015) 18 *Journal of International Law* 233.

[77] "Singapore", Global Food Security Index December 2019, online: <https://foodsecurityindex.eiu.com/Country/Details #Singapore>; Agri-Food & Veterinary Authority of Singapore, "Singapore's Food Security", online: <https://agrifood.net/images/ cfs43/CFS43%20Side-event%20background%20document%20- %20Lessons%20from%20Singapore.pdf>.

restrictions on food exports, leading quickly to reciprocal action by other countries, and even further increases in world grain prices, seriously impairing the welfare of countries with limited domestic food production capacity. Means tested subsidies on the demand side, such as food stamps appropriately calibrated to prevailing prices, may have been a better targeted response and avoided the beggar-my-neighbour, zero sum character of many of the prevailing responses.

VI. The coronavirus pandemic and international trade policy

As of August 2020, the coronavirus has infected more than 18 million people and taken more than 700,000 lives. Some estimates suggest that at least 40 percent of the world's people will become infected, with millions of deaths, before the pandemic runs its course.[1] The scale and nature of this pandemic has generated a great deal of uncertainty regarding its long-term impact on the health of individuals, health systems, and the global economy. Some commentators portend the end of globalization as we have known it.[2] As to long-term predictions, I take seriously the wisdom of John Kenneth Galbraith's quip that economic forecasting makes astrology look respectable, to which I would add that any form of long-term forecasting, particularly forecasts made in the midst of a global healthcare calamity, are entitled to very little credibility, and I make no such predictions myself. In the midst of this crisis and dealing with day-to-day decisions that must be made in the light of rapidly changing local conditions, the time is not appropriate

---

[1]   Nicholas A. Christakis, "Nicholas Christakis on Fighting Covid-19 by Truly Understanding the Virus", *The Economist* (August 10, 2020), online: <https://www.economist.com/by-invitation/2020/08/10/nicholas-christakis-on-fighting-covid-19-by-truly-understanding-the-virus>.

[2]   Kenneth Rapoza, "The Post-Coronavirus World May Be the End of Globalization", *Forbes* (April 3, 2020), online: <https://www.forbes.com/sites/kenrapoza/2020/04/03/the-post-coronavirus-world-may-be-the-end-of-globalization>. See Fareed Zakaria, Ten Lessons for the Post-Pandemic World (W.W. Norton, 2020), chap. 8.

for drawing strong long-term lessons as to how to deal most effectively with such a crisis. Nevertheless, with the increasing amount of information that we do have, it is possible to take preliminary steps in examining the health and economic dimensions of the pandemic and assessing potential solutions.

A)   THE HEALTH DIMENSION OF THE CORONAVIRUS PANDEMIC

First, the nature of the coronavirus makes its spread extremely difficult to contain and control. While the overall fatality rate of the virus is relatively low, the virus is carried by a large portion of the population, and the chances of becoming infected are high. Some people might have no symptoms at all but still carry the virus and have the ability to transmit the virus to others. Even for those who develop symptoms, the symptoms generally take around seven days to show, although the patient can begin spreading the disease two to four days before they become symptomatic.[3] In addition, particularly because the virus leads to mild symptoms for many of those who are infected, there is a tendency for the public and politicians to take it less seriously, again making the disease harder to control.[4]

In terms of treatment, because the virus can cause a wide range of symptoms that vary in type and severity among patients, there is no standard treatment package available for the disease. While some might have only mild symptoms, others have severe complications that require hospitalization.[5] And while many have symptoms that last only a short amount

---

[3]   Nicholas A. Christakis, "Nicholas Christakis on Fighting Covid-19 by Truly Understanding the Virus".

[4]   Nicholas A. Christakis, "Nicholas Christakis on Fighting Covid-19 by Truly Understanding the Virus".

[5]   The Economist, "When Covid-19 Becomes a Chronic Illness", *The Economist* (22 August 2020), online: <https://www.economist

of time, a small but significant proportion of those infected have symptoms that last for months.[6] In terms of the complications that the coronavirus can cause, it is now clear that the virus does not only attack the lungs and the respiratory system but can also damage the heart and possibly even the brain and central nervous system.[7] Facing such a wide array of symptoms and few detailed explanations of exactly how the virus behaves, much uncertainty remains despite increasing bodies of data produced by studies in the US, UK, China, and Europe as thousands of patients are being observed and treated.[8]

Because of the characteristics of the coronavirus, the pandemic has caused severe disruption to health systems around the world. An important area where these negative impacts are most evident is primary healthcare. For example, disruptive effects are seen in prenatal care, family medicine, elective surgeries, and routine childhood immunization.[9] Moreover, the coronavirus pandemic has also caused severe disruptions in health services for noncommunicable diseases (NCDs). This situation is serious because people living with NCDs are at a higher risk of developing severe symptoms if they become infected with the coronavirus. In a recent WHO survey of 155 countries, a substantial number of countries reported disrupted services for treatments for NCDs such as hypertension, diabetes, cancer, and cardiovascular emergencies. In the majority of countries, healthcare staff previously working in the area of

---

.com/science-and-technology/2020/08/22/when-covid-19-becomes-a-chronic-illness>.

[6]   Gavi, "The Long-term Health Effects of COVID-19", *Gavi* (June 19, 2020), online: <https://www.gavi.org/vaccineswork/long-term-health-effects-covid-19>.

[7]   The Economist, "When Covid-19 Becomes a Chronic Illness".

[8]   The Economist, "When Covid-19 Becomes a Chronic Illness".

[9]   Maria Cohut, "How the Pandemic has Affected Primary Healthcare around the World", *Medical News Today* (May 15, 2020), online: <https://www.medicalnewstoday.com/articles/how-the-pandemic-has-affected-primary-healthcare-around-the-world>.

NCDs were partially or fully reassigned to support COVID-19 related work. Overall, low-income countries are affected most by these disruptions. While 72 percent of high-income countries reported that they had included NCD services in their national COVID-19 plans, only 42 percent of low-income countries had.[10]

B)   THE ECONOMIC DIMENSION OF THE CORONAVIRUS PANDEMIC

Beyond these health-related disruptions, there are also severe economic implications of the pandemic. Because of the borderless nature of the coronavirus, this global pandemic has put a larger proportion of the global community in economic recession than at any other time since the Great Depression. The World Bank recently predicted that the global economy will shrink by 5.2 percent in 2020, and that the pandemic will push around 60 million people into extreme poverty. Using broader measures including the lack of basic shelter, food, and clean water, the UN predicts that the number of poor people will increase by 240 to 490 million in 2020.[11] The IMF has predicted that the deficit-to-GDP ratio will increase from 3.3 percent in 2019 to 16.6 percent in 2020 for advanced economies, and from 4.9 percent to 10.6 percent for emerging economies. In a significant number of countries, the pan-

---

[10]   World Health Organization, "COVID-19 Significantly Impacts Health Services for Noncommunicable Diseases", *World Health Organization* (June 1, 2020), online: <https://www.who.int/news-room/detail/01-06-2020-covid-19-significantly-impacts-health-services-for-noncommunicable-diseases>.

[11]   The Economist, "Failing the Poor: COVID-19 Has Reversed Years of Gains in the War on Poverty", *The Economist* (September 26, 2020), online: <https://www.economist.com/leaders/2020/09/26/covid-19-has-reversed-years-of-gains-in-the-war-on-poverty>.

demic has already created a massive economic contraction.[12] Unemployment has also increased and will likely continue to increase. For example, the US has recorded the worst monthly unemployment figures in 72 years, and the Bank of England warned that in 2020 the UK will face its steepest decline in output since 1706.[13]

Carmen and Vincent Reinhart have recently summarized several indicators suggesting that an economic recovery is likely to be slow and difficult.[14] The first indicator is exports. Even before the pandemic, global trade growth was on a decreasing trend, which was intensified by the recent US–China trade conflict. The pandemic has led to the closure of borders and lockdowns, and as a result has further decreased the global demand for goods. Export-dependent economies have been hit especially hard. The second indicator is unemployment. Because the pandemic and the resulting lockdowns closed the doors of many businesses temporarily or permanently, employment is likely to take a long time to rebound. Some workers will end up leaving the labour force permanently, and others will miss out on professional development opportunities during their time of unemployment which makes them less attractive to potential employers. A severe impact is also likely to be experienced by recent graduates entering an impaired economy. Moreover, many of those still in school may receive substandard education in online classrooms and in some countries that lack internet infrastructure, marginalized and poor students may end up leaving the education system

---

[12] Carmen Reinhart and Vincent Reinhart, "The Pandemic Depression: The Global Economy Will Never Be the Same", *Foreign Affairs* (2020), online: <https://www.foreignaffairs.com/print/node/1126226>.

[13] Carmen Reinhart and Vincent Reinhart, "The Pandemic Depression: The Global Economy Will Never Be the Same".

[14] Carmen Reinhart and Vincent Reinhart, "The Pandemic Depression: The Global Economy Will Never Be the Same".

altogether, creating a cohort of left-behind school-aged children and teens.[15] The third indicator is the regressive nature of the pandemic, with its ongoing economic disruptions falling hardest on the poor. Those with lower incomes are generally less able to work remotely and have less resources at their disposal when they are not working. In developing countries with underdeveloped social safety nets, the decline in living standards will fall most heavily on the poorest segments of the population. These disruptions may also be intensified with a global spike in food prices since diseases and lockdowns disrupt supply chains and agricultural production. The United Nations has recently warned that the world is facing the worst food crisis in 50 years. People in low-income countries spend a much larger share of their income on food and thus the food crisis will further intensify the already disproportionate economic impact of the pandemic on the most disadvantaged.[16]

Finally, the pandemic's economic impact is particularly severe for developing countries and least developed countries (LDCs). The congested living conditions in many parts of the developing world, such as slums and refugee camps, make social distancing and self isolation particularly difficult, if not impossible. In addition, high poverty levels force people to go out and work. A large proportion of workers in developing countries work in informal employment with low wages. Not only is it impossible to work from home for most of these jobs, but any economic lockdown measure would immediately lead to deeper poverty and hunger.[17] Many developing countries also have poor healthcare infrastructure and are thus

---

[15] Carmen Reinhart and Vincent Reinhart, "The Pandemic Depression: The Global Economy Will Never Be the Same".

[16] Carmen Reinhart and Vincent Reinhart, "The Pandemic Depression: The Global Economy Will Never Be the Same".

[17] UN, "COVID-19: Impact Could Cause Equivalent of 195 Million Job Losses, Says ILO Chief", *UN News* (April 8, 2020), online: <https://news.un.org/en/story/2020/04/1061322>.

less capable of dealing with the impact of the pandemic. On average, there are only 113 hospital beds per 100,000 inhabitants in LDCs, which is less than half of the number in other developing countries and 80 percent below developed countries. Moreover, for many LDCs and developing countries, even the most basic measures such as frequent handwashing are difficult for their citizens.[18] In addition, the weak fiscal capacity of many developing countries makes it difficult for them to provide income safety nets. While governments of developed countries spent more than 10 percent of their GDP to ease the economic pain, emerging economies have only spent 3 percent and the poorest nations not even 1 percent. Furthermore, many governments in poor countries have spent the majority of their money helping corporate giants rather than the poor. For example, since the crisis, Mexico provided their large oil company tax breaks worth $2.7 billion, but no new programmes for the poor. In countries like South Africa and Uganda, funds meant for alleviating effects of the pandemic have not been able to reach those who need it the most due to fraud and corruption.[19] Finally, even for developing countries that have been able to implement effective measures to mitigate the worst short term impacts of the crisis and are thus less likely to face a recession, they are still unlikely to escape devastating long-term impacts such as damage to their trading relations, decreasing returns on investment, and a significant loss of human capital due to disruptions in education.[20]

---

[18]   UN, "UN/DESA Policy Brief #66: Covid-19 and the Least Developed Countries", *UN* (1 May 2020), online: <https://www.un.org/development/desa/dpad/publication/un-desa-policy-brief-66-covid-19-and-the-least-developed-countries/>.

[19]   The Economist, "Failing the Poor: COVID-19 Has Reversed Years of Gains in the War on Poverty".

[20]   The Economist, "In Emerging Markets, Short-term Panic Gives Way to Long-term Worry", *The Economist* (August 1, 2020), online: <https://www.economist.com/finance-and-economics/2020/

C) INTERNATIONAL TRADE AND THE PANDEMIC

During the current global pandemic and economic recession, issues relating to medical equipment and vaccine security have loomed large in contemporary public and policy discussions. These concerns have raised a host of implications for international trade policy. First, on the export side, many countries are restricting exports of essential medical supplies in an attempt to keep these supplies at home (as Article XI of the GATT may permit on a temporary basis). Second, on the import side, countries are attempting to increase domestic self-sufficiency by either restricting imports or subsidizing domestic producers. Third, intellectual property protection in the international trade regime threatens a replay of the HIV/AIDS controversy in the 1990s by possibly denying low-income developing countries access to essential vaccines and antivirals under patents once they become available.

1)   Export Restrictions

First, as in the run-up in world grain prices in 2007–2008, countries understandably will wish to reserve essential medical equipment as a first priority for their own citizens. Hence, we currently observe a number of countries restricting exports of essential medical equipment and other countries responding in kind. For example, in the early months of the coronavirus pandemic, countries like China, France, Germany, and the US hoarded supplies of respirators, surgical masks, and gloves for their own hospitals and people. Similarly, the leader of the US supply chain response to COVID-19, Peter Navarro, stated that "if we have learned anything from the coronavirus and

---

08/01/in-emerging-markets-short-term-panic-gives-way-to-long-term-worry>.

swine flu H1N1 epidemic of 2009, it is that we cannot necessarily depend on other countries, even close allies, to supply us with needed items, from face masks to vaccines."[21] Shortly after this statement, the Trump Administration imposed export restrictions, including to many poor countries, on surgical masks, respirators, and gloves. Overall, more than 70 countries have imposed export controls on medical equipment, personal protective equipment, and medicines.[22]

The imposition of export restrictions in an attempt to reserve essential medical supplies for one's own country is not only ineffective but also counterproductive in the long run. As Chad Bown of the Peterson Institute has extensively documented,[23] many countries are simultaneously both exporters and importers of essential medical equipment or its components, so that severe and enduring restrictions on medical equipment exports are likely to engender a beggar-my-neighbour zero sum dynamic, leaving all countries worse off in the long run. One example that illustrates these risks is the EU's March 2020 export restriction policy which limits an estimated $12.1 billion worth of medical equipment exports (including face shields, protective garments, mouth-nose-protective equipment, hospital gloves, and protective spectacles and

---

[21]   Thomas J. Bollyky and Chad P. Bown, "The Tragedy of Vaccine Nationalism: Only Cooperation can End the Pandemic", *Foreign Affairs* (July 27, 2020).

[22]   Thomas J. Bollyky and Chad P. Bown, "The Tragedy of Vaccine Nationalism: Only Cooperation can End the Pandemic".

[23]   Chad P. Bown, "EU Limits on Medical Gear Exports Put Poor Countries and Europeans at Risk", *Peterson Institute for International Economics Blogs* (March 19, 2020), online: <www.piie.com>; Chad P. Bown, "China's Exports of Protective Medical Equipment Fell Less than Its Exports of All Other Products", *Peterson Institute for International Economics Blogs* (March 30, 2020), online: <www.piie.com>; Chad P. Bown, "COVID-19: Trump's Curbs on Exports of Medical Gear Put Americans and Others at Risk", *Peterson Institute for International Economics Blogs* (April 9, 2020), online: <www.piie.com>.

visors). One consequence of these policies is that they would make the EU vulnerable to other countries' retaliatory export restrictions, as the EU is not only an exporter but simultaneously also an importer of these medical supplies. In 2019, the EU imported $17.6 billion worth of the products on which it has currently imposed export controls. Thus, if countries affected by the EU's policies respond in kind, EU member countries could be cut off from their access to global markets for essential medical imports. For example, under normal circumstances, 9 percent of the EU's exports of face shields go to Switzerland, and at the same time, Switzerland supplies 7 percent of the EU's imports of face shields. Yet as a result of the EU's export restrictions, Swiss hospital workers would be forced to utilize local suppliers of face shields, and thus reduce the availability of Swiss face shields for export and in turn hurt EU member states themselves.

In addition, the EU could be faced with retaliatory export restrictions on *other* medical products. For example, a country affected by the EU's export restrictions on face shields may retaliate by restricting its exports to the EU of other essential equipment such as ventilators, X-ray equipment, or syringes. This would again engender harm to the EU itself, as the EU imports $8.8 billion of these critical medical supplies from the rest of the world. In addition, EU export restrictions would leave many poor countries that depend on imports of medical supplies from the EU vulnerable, including countries in Eastern Europe, northern Africa, and sub-Saharan Africa. In the Central African Republic, for example, 100 percent of its imports of protective spectacles and visors are sourced from the EU. In Greenland, Cape Verde, and Andorra, more than 90 percent of imports of face shields are also sourced from the EU. Unfortunately, the EU's regulation provided no safeguards to ensure that the poorest countries with few available alternatives are not cut off during the pandemic.[24]

2)   Import Restrictions and Subsidies

A related concern is that countries have become too dependent on foreign suppliers of essential medical supplies so that they run the risk of being held to ransom when essential medical equipment is in global short supply. Thus, many countries are aiming to attain high levels of domestic self-sufficiency in essential medical supplies through import restrictions or subsidies. For example, a prominent scientist and former chairman of the Indian Space Research Organisation recently argued that India should aim to become self-reliant in the field of medical equipment and devices.[25] Similarly, Italy's national commissioner for the pandemic emergency stated that Italy hopes to become self-sufficient in producing protective masks. The commissioner argued that the reason for difficulties during the pandemic was that "there is no made-in-Italy production of the ammunition we need to fight this war".[26]

---

[24]   Chad P. Bown, "EU Limits on Medical Gear Exports Put Poor Countries and Europeans at Risk"; Chad P. Bown, "China's Exports of Protective Medical Equipment Fell Less than Its Exports of All Other Products", Chad P. Bown, "COVID-19: Trump's Curbs on Exports of Medical Gear Put Americans and Others at Risk".

[25]   India Times, "India Should Become Self-reliant in Medical Equipment, Devices: Kasturirangan", *India Times* (April 10, 2020), online: <https://health.economictimes.indiatimes.com/news/medical-devices/india-should-become-self-reliant-in-medical-equipmentdevices-kasturirangan/75082746>.

[26]   Elvira Pollina, "Italy Sees Self-Sufficiency in Mask Production against Coronavirus in Two Months", *The Chronicle Herald* (March 24, 2020), online: <https://www.thechronicleherald.ca/news/world/italy-sees-self-sufficiency-in-mask-production-against-coronavirus-in-two-months-428783>.

I am sceptical of the merits of the argument that in the longer term countries should aim to achieve much higher levels of domestic self-sufficiency in essential medical equipment, along the same lines of arguments discussed earlier for self-sufficiency in the production of essential foodstuffs. As in the case of essential foodstuffs, domestic self-sufficiency in essential medical equipment or supplies poses its own risks in the event that a major health crisis predominantly or disproportionately strikes a country wholly or largely dependent on its own suppliers and lacking established networks of suppliers in other countries.

Just as a prudent retirement investment strategy is likely to entail investing in a widely diversified portfolio of securities, so it makes sense in the case of essential medical supplies to diversify broadly sources of supply, as in the striking case of Singapore with respect to food security, complemented by a strategy of maintaining ample domestic buffer stocks of essential medical supplies that may be required in the event of a major health crisis. Thus, diversifying risks of shortages in supply over both place and time has many advantages over draconian and mutually destructive export restrictions, or import restrictions designed to promote exclusive reliance on often higher cost domestic industries that are unlikely to possess adequate production capacity in the face of a major domestic health crisis. Moreover, subsidies to local producers of medical supplies to reduce dependency on foreign suppliers may provoke international trade disputes under the prohibition on local sourcing subsidies in the Subsidies and Countervailing Measures Agreement, National Treatment commitments in the Government Procurement Agreement, or similar commitments under the Trade-Related Investment Measures Agreement.

3)   IP Protection and Access to Vaccines

A third issue that is likely to arise relates to access to vaccines and antivirals once they are developed. Currently, as candidate vaccines are being developed and tested, countries have already began competing for early access to these vaccines once they are approved. For example, the CEO of Sanofi, a French-based biopharmaceutical company, stated that the US "has the right to the largest pre-order" of vaccines due to an investment agreement signed between the company and US government agencies. Similarly, a UK pharmaceutical company reported that the first 30 million doses of the vaccine that it is developing will be allocated to the UK itself, due to the UK government's financial investment. Subsequently, the US pledged $1.2 billion USD to the company to obtain 300 million doses of the vaccine, as part of President Trump's Operation Warp Speed for obtaining vaccines for Americans as early as possible. These kinds of actions recall events from earlier pandemics such as the 2009 H1N1 pandemic. When a vaccine was developed for the virus, rich countries looked to domestic pharmaceutical companies for production and directly negotiated with them for large pre-orders of the vaccine, which ended up crowding out poor countries. As a result, distribution of the H1N1 vaccine was based not on scientific evidence about the risk of transmission, but on the purchasing power of high-income countries.[27]

Thus, it is likely that governments will continue to prioritize taking care of their own populations over slowing the global spread of the coronavirus or helping the most vulnerable. This kind of "vaccine nationalism" will likely lead to a bidding war between rich countries, drive up the price of vaccines,

---

[27] Rebecca Weintraub, Asaf Bitton, and Mark L. Rosenberg, "The Danger of Vaccine Nationalism", *Harvard Business Review* (May 22, 2020), online: <https://hbr.org/2020/05/the-danger-of-vaccine-nationalism>.

and make them virtually inaccessible to poorer countries. This will result in vulnerable populations in low and middle income countries having to wait months or longer for their vaccination supply, extending the length of the pandemic, its death toll, and its negative impact on fragile health systems and economies. Furthermore, because today's vaccine supply chains are inevitably global, some countries might search for leverage, for example, by blocking the export of critical vaccine components such as raw ingredients, syringes, and vials. In other cases, countries might also strike short term deals for vaccines that are damaging to their economies in the long run.[28] Most importantly, if the virus continues to spread in a country that was unable to obtain vaccines and other essential medical supplies, the disease will continue to spread globally and endanger people and economies around the world. In June 2020, organizations including the United Nations and the International Red Cross declared that it was a "moral imperative" that everyone have access to a "people's vaccine".[29] Unfortunately, these kinds of declarations are not enforceable, and global vaccine allocation is likely to prove a daunting challenge.

Issues related to access to vaccines, particularly for poor developing countries, are further complicated by intellectual property (IP) rights protections in the international trade regime. IP protections raise the possibility of a replay of controversial events seen during the 1990s AIDS pandemic. As discussed in the IP section of this book, the 1995 TRIPS Agreement provided strong intellectual property rights pro-tections to pharmaceutical companies in developed countries

---

[28]   Thomas J. Bollyky and Chad P. Bown, "The Tragedy of Vaccine Nationalism: Only Cooperation Can End The Pandemic".

[29]   Maria Cheng and Christina Larson, "As Rich Nations Prepare for Coronavirus Vaccine, Others Could Be Left Behind: Experts", *Global News* (June 18, 2020), online: <https://globalnews.ca/news/7079365/coronavirus-vaccines-countries>.

which developed and manufactured essential treatments for the AIDS pandemic. Patented medicines had high price tags, which were unattainable for poor developing countries that needed the treatments most. The devastating effect of developing countries' lack of access to lifesaving treatments led to the clarification of the TRIPS Agreement's flexibilities for developing countries in 2001 through the Doha Declaration on the TRIPS Agreement and Public Health and subsequent amendments to TRIPS. Specifically, it was clarified that Article 31 of the TRIPS Agreement gave countries the right to grant compulsory licences, which allows a government to locally manufacture generic versions of the treatment without the patent holder's consent. In Clause 5 of the Doha Declaration, it was affirmed that countries have the "right to grant compulsory licenses and the freedom to determine the grounds upon which such licenses are granted". In addition, in situations of national emergency, governments can issue compulsory licences without normal requirements such as negotiating with the patent holder.[30] Thus, developing countries could determine for themselves if they were facing a national emergency such as a public health crisis, and issue compulsory licences to locally manufacture generic versions of the treatment without negotiating with the patent holder.[31] As noted earlier, the requirement of payment of "adequate remuneration" to the patent holder is vague and has never been clarified.

If access to vaccines remains difficult due to vaccine nationalism and the absence of a global vaccine agreement

---

[30] Hilary Wong, "The Case for Compulsory Licensing during COVID-19" (2020) 10 *Journal of Global Health*, online: <https://www.ncbi.nlm.nih.gov/pmc/articles/PMC7242884>.

[31] Dianne Nicol and Olasupo Owoeye, "Using TRIPS Flexibilities to Facilitate Access to Medicines", *Bulletin of the World Health Organization* (2013), online: <https://www.who.int/bulletin/volumes/91/7/12-115865/en>.

addressing equitable distribution and financing of vaccines, there is a strong possibility that developing countries will take unilateral actions. For example, developing countries with a significant generic drug industry, such as China, India, and Brazil, might invoke the TRIPS Agreement's compulsory licensing provisions. Smaller developing countries without generic drug manufacturing capacities would likely enter into compulsory licensing agreements with larger developing countries with such capacities to obtain vaccines and treatments at more accessible prices (as amendments to TRIPS permit). Such unilateral actions are likely to intensify trade conflicts, exacerbating already severe dislocations of international trade.

D)   POTENTIAL SOLUTIONS

In response to the wide array of challenging issues raised by the global pandemic, scholars and commentators have proposed a series of potential solutions. In addressing issues of access to medical equipment and vaccines, Bollyky and Bown emphasize the need for global cooperation in the form of an international COVID-19 vaccine trade and investment agreement, and an enforceable commitment to distribute vaccines globally in an equitable and rational way. As Bollyky and Bown argue, such an agreement could be created by existing institutions, and could be enforced by the dynamics of global trade, which generate layers of interdependence that would motivate countries to comply with their commitments. Yet as the world gets closer to the first effective vaccine, there will be less time to set up such an agreement. Thus, sooner rather than later, political leaders from the majority of vaccine-manufacturing countries will need to instruct their respective health and trade ministers to take the first step of working together to create a short term agreement that outlines the conditions for the allocation of vaccines. This initial step could then convince more countries, with the fear of missing out on vaccine access, to sign on, leading to a global cooperative deal on vaccine allocation, which would be the most efficient way to curb the spread of the virus and limit the virus's toll on human lives.[32] The potential for unilateral action by many countries under the amended compulsory licensing provision of the TRIPS Agreement may provide major incentives to reach such an agreement. The Covax public-private partnership initiative, anchored by the World Health Organization, is a promising development in this direction.

Beyond the allocation of vaccines, some scholars have also advocated the implementation of financial measures in poor countries. For example, commentators from *The Economist* have suggested that the best way to help the poor is to give them money directly since this kind of simple cash transfer is less vulnerable to corruption, and can provide immediate help to families who need to feed their children and send them back to school.[33] Similarly, Esther Duflo and Abhijit Banerjee have proposed that poor countries should implement a "universal ultra basic income" (UUBI) programme.[34] This proposal reflects a recognition that health systems in many developing countries are poorly equipped to deal with the pandemic, and poverty is often a cause of a higher risk of serious illness.

---

[32]   Thomas J. Bollyky and Chad P. Bown, "The Tragedy of Vaccine Nationalism: Only Cooperation Can End the Pandemic".

[33]   The Economist, "Failing the Poor: COVID-19 Has Reversed Years of Gains in the War on Poverty".

[34]   Esther Duflo and Abhijit Banerjee, "Coronavirus Is a Crisis for the Developing World, but Here's Why It Needn't Be a Catastrophe," *The Guardian* (May 6, 2020), online: <https://www.theguardian.com/commentisfree/2020/may/06/vulnerable-countries-poverty-deadly-coronavirus-crisis>; Abhijit Banerjee and Esther Duflo, "Abhijit Banerjee and Esther Duflo on How Economies Can Rebound", *The Economist* (May 26, 2020), online: <https://www.economist.com/by-invitation/2020/05/26/abhijit-banerjee-and-esther-duflo-on-how-economies-can-rebound>.

While many poor countries have taken an extremely cautious approach by imposing severe lockdowns in response to the pandemic, quarantine measures cannot last forever, and the countries need to balance the need to control the spread of the virus and the need to kickstart their economic recovery post-lockdown. In these circumstances, low-income countries, through the UUBI, could provide a regular cash transfer that allows for basic survival among their citizens. This kind of cash transfer carries the virtues of simplicity, transparency, and an assurance that nobody will starve. Particularly during a pandemic, the simplicity of this kind of transfer could lead to lifesaving results. In addition, many developing countries, particularly in Africa, already have existing infrastructure in place for rapid transfers of money across the population via mobile phones.

However, these financial measures are out of reach for many low-income developing countries. As Duflo and Banerjee point out, the greatest constraint to implementation of this scheme is not its feasibility, but political and financial willpower. Many developing countries are facing increasing financial pressure as they not only need to provide basic financial support for their population, but also need to buy essentials such as food and medical supplies, test enough people on a systematic basis to determine when and where a reopening of the economy is possible, and support the healthcare system to avert its collapse. The cost of these measures will likely be out of reach for most low-income developing countries. While governments in developed countries and richer developing countries can provide safety nets for their citizens in the short run since they can borrow money at a cheap rates, poor developing countries do not have access to international credit markets at low rates because they are often already highly indebted. For example, in most of Africa, these measures are unattainable without external financial support and debt forgiveness. Poor countries cannot manage the crisis on their own, and implementing these measures would require substantial financial help from richer countries. So far, rich countries have done little to help. In this context, Banerjee and Duflo propose a "Covid-19 Marshall Plan" for low-income countries, which involves financial support from developed countries, in addition to their help in cooperating with international financial institutions on debt relief.[35]

---

[35] Esther Duflo and Abhijit Banerjee, "Coronavirus Is a Crisis for the Developing World, but Here's Why It Needn't Be a Catastrophe"; Abhijit Banerjee and Esther Duflo, "Abhijit Banerjee and Esther Duflo on How Economies Can Rebound".

VII. The US–China trade conflict

As outlined in earlier chapters, several issues lie at the root of the China–US trade conflict, including concerns about persistent US trade deficits with China, China's subsidies to its state owned enterprises, currency manipulation for competitive advantage, weak intellectual property protection, and forced technology transfer from foreign firms. While some of these issues are longstanding concerns in China–US trade relations, the US Trump Administration has taken a more aggressive stance towards China's trade practices. The beginning of the US–China trade war can be traced to March 2018 when the Office of the US Trade Representative (USTR) published its Section 301 investigation, which documents some of China's trade-distorting practices.[1] Since 2018, the Trump Administration has imposed tariffs on more than $300 billion of imports from China, and the average tariff rate increased from 2.7 percent to 17.5 percent. In response, China's retaliatory tariffs increased the average tariff rate on US exports from 5.7 percent to 20.4 percent.[2] As a result, the trade war has

---

[1]   Virgil Bisio, Charles Horne, Ann Listerud, Kaj Malden, Leyton Nelson, Nargiza Salidjanova, and Suzanna Stephens, "The US-China 'Phase One' Deal: A Backgrounder", *US-China Economic and Security Review Commission* (February 4, 2020), online: <https://www.uscc.gov/sites/default/files/2020-02/U.S.-China%20Trade%20Deal%20Issue%20Brief.pdf>.

[2]   Mary Amiti, Sang Hoon Kong, and David E. Weinstein, "The Investment Cost of the US-China Trade War," *Liberty Street Economics* (May 28, 2020), online: <https://libertystreeteconomics.newyorkfed.org/2020/05/the-investment-cost-of-the-us-china-trade-war.html>.

led to heavy economic costs for both countries, and has so far achieved little in realizing the aims of addressing fundamental conflicts at the root of China–US trade relations.

A) IMPACT OF THE TRADE WAR

1) Economic Impact of the Trade War in the US

While there have been a number of studies on the impact of the trade war and a range of estimates on its precise effect on GDP, most studies indicate that there has already been, and will continue to be, a significant loss to the US economy. For example, a study from September 2019 found that the trade war had already cost the US around 0.3 percent of real GDP. Other studies estimate a loss of up to 0.7 percent of US GDP.[3] The IMF estimates that US tariffs will decrease real GDP every year in the US up until 2023, by which time real GDP will be 0.5 percent lower than what it would have been without these tariffs. While a decrease of less than a percentage point in GDP may not seem significant, this impact translates to substantial losses for the US economy. In dollar terms, it is estimated that the trade war had already cost the US $134 billion by mid to end 2019, and $316 billion by the end of 2020.[4]

In addition, many studies find that the costs of the trade war have fallen primarily on American companies and consumers.

---

[3]   Ryan Hass and Abraham Denmark, "More Pain than Gain: How the US-China Trade War Hurt America," *Brookings* (August 7, 2020), online: <https://www.brookings.edu/blog/order-from-chaos/ 2020/08/07/more-pain-than-gain-how-the-us-china-trade-war-hurt -america>.

[4]   Shawn Donnan and Reade Pickert, "Trump's China Buying Spree Unlikely to Cover Trade War's Costs", *Bloomberg* (December 18, 2019), online: <https://www.bloomberg.com/news/articles/2019 -12-18/trump-s-china-buying-spree-unlikely-to-cover-trade-war-s -costs>.

An estimated $46 billion was paid by American companies as US tariffs forced companies to lower their profit margins, cut wages, cut jobs, and raise prices for consumers.[5] Recent research from the Federal Reserve Bank of New York and Columbia University found that US companies also lost at least $1.7 trillion in stock prices due to US tariffs on Chinese imports.[6] Furthermore, the uncertainty created by the trade war has also had a significant impact on business investment. A recent study estimates that the trade war had reduced US investment growth by 0.3 percent by the end of 2019, and was projected to decrease investment growth by another 1.6 percent by the end of 2020.[7] As a consequence of the damage to American businesses, an estimated 340,000 jobs were lost by the third quarter of 2019, due to the trade war's tariffs and its negative impact on investment.[8]

For consumers, the costs of the trade war are being paid in the form of higher prices on goods from China. In 2018, the US imported $539 billion worth of Chinese goods, which is equivalent to 21 percent of the value of all American imports. Many Chinese goods, such as cell phones, computers, toys, apparel, household appliances, and furniture, are essential everyday products for American consumers. Recent research found that the American consumer, as a result of the trade war, is expected to pay $1.6 billion more per year for house-

---

[5]   Andrea Shalal, "Trump's Tariffs Cost US Companies $46 Billion to Date, Data Shows", *Reuters* (January 9, 2020), online: <https://www.reuters.com/article/us-usa-trade-economy/trumps-tariffs-cost-u-s-companies-46-billion-to-date-data-shows-idUSKBN1Z8222>.

[6]   Ryan Hass and Abraham Denmark, "More Pain than Gain: How the US-China Trade War Hurt America".

[7]   Mary Amiti, Sang Hoon Kong, and David E. Weinstein, "The Investment Cost of the US-China Trade War".

[8]   Shawn Donnan and Reade Pickert, "Trump's China Buying Spree Unlikely to Cover Trade War's Costs".

hold appliances and $4.6 billion more for furniture.[9] A 2019 study estimated that trade war tariffs would translate into an additional cost of $831 per household per year, amounting to an annual cost of more than $106 billion for the US economy as a whole.[10]

Moreover, it is easy to be misled by statistics showing that protectionist tariffs save jobs in a particular industry, as the Trump Administration has claimed in support of its policies. First, jobs that are saved or created in a particular industry often come at the expense of job losses elsewhere. Since Trump's tariffs were announced in 2018, it is true that new jobs were added to the US economy, particularly in the manufacturing and steel sectors. However, these tariffs at the same time hurt employment in other sectors.[11] For example, after Trump's steel tariffs were announced, an increase of roughly 1,000 jobs in steel-producing industries was seen by November 2019, yet the larger industries that depend on imported steel, such as automakers and construction groups, have suffered. The increase in the cost of steel has also put US exporters at a disadvantage since they must compete with foreign companies paying lower steel prices. As a result, industries that use steel most intensively were at the highest risk of job losses. One study estimated that by mid-2019,

---

[9]   Prerana Priyadarshi, "Caught in the Crossfire: American Consumers and the US-China Trade War", *The Wire* (September 29, 2019), online: <https://thewire.in/world/american-consumer-us-china-trade-war>.

[10]   Mary Amiti, Stephen J. Redding, and David E. Weinstein, "New China Tariffs Increase Costs to US Households", *Liberty Street Economics* (May 23, 2019), online: <https://libertystreeteconomics.newyorkfed.org/2019/05/new-china-tariffs-increase-costs-to-us-households.html>.

[11]   Jeffrey Kucik, "Is Trump's Trade War Saving American Jobs – Or Killing Them?" *The Conversation* (May 15, 2019), online: <https://theconversation.com/is-trumps-trade-war-saving-american-jobs-or-killing-them-117159>.

increased costs due to the steel tariffs were associated with 0.6 percent fewer jobs in the manufacturing sector, amounting to about 75,000 job losses.[12]

In addition, jobs created or saved by tariffs can also be of enormous cost to consumers in terms of higher prices, and the additional costs to consumers are often much larger relative to the value of jobs saved. For example, in the case of the 2018 tariffs on washing machines, economists at the University of Chicago and Federal Reserve Board found that while these tariffs might have created 1,800 new jobs, this came at a sub-stantial cost to consumers who had to pay higher prices on washing machines and related items. Specifically, the tariffs increased consumer costs by around $1.5 billion, or more than $800,000 per US job created – 19 times greater than the value of the new jobs created.[13]

2)   Economic Costs of the Trade War for China

The most direct impact of the trade war on the Chinese economy is evident in the drop in exports. In 2019, Chinese exports to the US dropped by more than 12 percent[14] – a decrease of $35 billion in Chinese exports in the US

---

[12]   Lydia Cox and Kadee Russ, "Steel Tariffs and US Jobs Revisited", *Econofact* (February 6, 2020), online: <https://econofact.org/steel-tariffs-and-u-s-jobs-revisited>.

[13]   Mark J. Perry, "Trump's Washing Machine Tariffs Create 1,800 US Jobs, but At a YUGE Cost to Consumers of $820,000/Job," *AEI* (April 21, 2019), online: <https://www.aei.org/carpe-diem/trumps-washing-machine-tariffs-created-1800-us-jobs-but-at-a-yuge-cost-to-consumers-of-820000-job/>.

[14]   Alisa Chang, "Has the Trade War Taken a Bite out of China's Economy? Yes – But It's Complicated", *NPR* (October 10, 2019), online: <https://www.npr.org/2019/10/10/768569711/has-the-trade-war-taken-a-bite-out-of-china-s-economy-yes-but-its-complicated>.

market.[15] However, China compensated for much of its loss by increasing exports to other countries around the world. As a result, China's net exports in 2019 only decreased by $2.8 billion. For example, China's exports to Southeast Asia rose by $38.5 billion, and exports to Europe and Sub-Saharan Africa also increased. In addition, due to sharp declines in exports of processed manufactured goods to the US, China cut back on imports of component parts from Japan, South Korea and Taiwan. Added to the cuts in Chinese imports from the United States due to retaliatory tariffs, China experienced a substantial decline in total imports in 2019, which led to an improvement in China's trade balance by $60 billion despite the trade war.[16]

In terms of impact on Chinese consumers, Chinese economists estimate that while there will be a negative impact, it will not be as significant as those experienced by American consumers, largely because American products do not make up a large portion of essential goods for Chinese consumers. According to economist Wenling Chen,[17] for some everyday goods such as meat products imported from the US, Chinese consumers might face a steep price increase. However, for many others, the impact is much smaller. For example, soybeans imported from the US account for less than one third of Chinese supply of the product in its domestic market. In

---

[15]　UNCTAD, "Trade War Leaves Both US And China Worse Off," *UNCTAD* (November 6, 2019), online: <https://unctad.org/news/trade-war-leaves-both-us-and-china-worse>.

[16]　Yukon Huang and Jeremy Smith, "In US-China Trade War, New Supply Chains Rattle Markets", *Carnegie Endowment for International Peac*e (June 24, 2020), online: <https://carnegieendowment.org/2020/06/24/in-u.s.-china-trade-war-new-supply-chains-rattle-markets-pub-82145>.

[17]　Lian Jun, "What Impact Will the China-US Trade War Bring for Us? 中美贸易战会给我们带来多大影响？" *CE* (August 12, 2018), online: <http://www.ce.cn/xwzx/gnsz/gdxw/201808/12/t20180812_30006779.shtml>.

addition, American soybeans are used only for soybean oil production in China. Thus, Chinese tariffs may lead to an increase in the prices of cooking oil for the average consumer, although the impact on oil prices would only amount to an increase of a few RMB per kilogram.

3)   The Impact of the Trade War on Other Countries

In the short term, countries that make products affected by US tariffs are likely to benefit. Instead of buying from China, American companies would likely buy similar products from other countries not affected by tariffs. Vietnam would be a clear winner, along with Taiwan. Vietnam's exports to the US rose by 35 percent in 2019, equivalent to $17.5 billion. In addition, Europe and Mexico benefited from increased exports to the US. In 2019, US imports from Europe rose by $31.2 billion, and US imports from Mexico rose by $11.6 billion.[18]

However, many countries are also negatively affected by the trade war. Because China and the US are huge markets for goods, tariffs could mean that consumers and businesses in the two countries buy less from all over the world, leading to an overall decrease in global demand. Furthermore, tariffs could decrease demand for a wide range of products that are made in China, but the component parts of those products are manufactured elsewhere and exported to China. Thus, the economic pain of the trade war could be spread to multiple countries along the supply chain. While some of this impact could be offset by shifting the entire production chain outside

---

[18]   Klint Finley, "Trump's Trade War Isn't Just a US-China Problem", *Wired* (August 26, 2019), online: <https://www.wired.com/story/us-china-trade-war-spills-over>.

of China, building new factories and training new employees is likely to be a costly and protracted process.[19]

B)   THE PHASE ONE DEAL

On January 15, 2020, China and the US signed a Phase One trade agreement as part of the effort to ease trade tensions between the two countries. This agreement entered into force on February 14, 2020. The Phase One deal addresses several major areas of dispute including tariffs, intellectual property, technology transfer, trade in food and agricultural products, financial services, exchange rate matters, and trade expansion.[20]

1)   Tariff Reductions and Trade Expansion

First, the US made concessions in a series of tariff reductions announced around the time of the Phase One deal. For example, the Trump Administration agreed to lower the tariffs imposed in September 2019 from 15 percent to 7.5 percent on the announced $120 billion worth of US imports from China. In addition, the Trump Administration suspended planned tariffs on around $180 billion of US imports which were otherwise to come into effect in December 2019. Similarly, China also suspended additional tariffs which were to be

---

[19]   Klint Finley, "Trump's Trade War Isn't Just a US-China Problem".

[20]   US Trade Representative, *Economic and Trade Agreement between the Government of the United States of America and the Government of the People's Republic of China*, US Trade Representative (2020), online: <https://ustr.gov/sites/default/files/files/agreements/phase%20one%20agreement/Economic_And_Trade_Agreement_Between_The_United_States_And_China_Text .pdf>. See also: Virgil Bisio, Charles Horne, Ann Listerud, Kaj Malden, Leyton Nelson, Nargiza Salidjanova, and Suzanna Stephens, "The US-China 'Phase One' Deal: A Backgrounder".

implemented in December 2019, and continued to suspend retaliatory tariffs on US auto exports.

A centrepiece of the Phase One deal is an ambitious agreement to increase China's purchase of US products. Specifically, China committed to increase its purchases of US products in 2020 and 2021 by $200 billion from 2017 levels. This includes a $76.7 billion increase in 2020 and a $123.3 billion increase in 2021. By sector, China committed to purchase an additional $76.7 billion in manufactured goods, $52.4 billion in energy, $32 billion in agricultural goods, and $37.9 billion in services.[21]

In addition, chapter 3 of the agreement outlines China's commitment to reduce barriers to imports of US food and agricultural products. The annex of this chapter sets out steps that China will take to facilitate the import of dairy products, infant formulas, and beef, pork and poultry products, among others. In addition, on genetically modified products, China agreed to reduce the review and approval period to no more than 24 months, down from the current approval period of five to seven years.[22]

2)   Intellectual Property, Technology Transfer and Exchange Rate Policy

Beyond the commitments on tariff reductions and increased purchases of US products, the agreement also sets out a series of commitments in areas including intellectual property rights

---

[21]   Virgil Bisio, Charles Horne, Ann Listerud, Kaj Malden, Leyton Nelson, Nargiza Salidjanova, and Suzanna Stephens, "The US-China 'Phase One' Deal: A Backgrounder".

[22]   US Trade Representative, *Economic and Trade Agreement between the Government of the United States of America and the Government of the People's Republic of China*. See also: Virgil Bisio, Charles Horne, Ann Listerud, Kaj Malden, Leyton Nelson, Nargiza Salidjanova, and Suzanna Stephens, "The US-China 'Phase One' Deal: A Backgrounder".

protection, forced technology transfer, and exchange rate policy.

Chapter 1 of the agreement addresses the issue of intellectual property. Here, China has committed to putting in place procedural changes that bring its IP administration in line with norms of other developed countries. These changes include shifting the burden of proof from the plaintiff to the defendant in civil proceedings for trade secret theft once the plaintiff meets a minimum evidentiary threshold; moving cases from administrative to criminal courts if there is a reasonable suspicion of criminal IP violations; providing for patent terms to be extended where the patent approval process entails regulatory delay; eliminating burdensome consular verifications of evidence presented in IP cases; and enumerating additional acts for trade secret misappropriation, among others.[23]

On technology transfer, addressed in chapter 2 of the Phase One agreement, China agreed to refrain from conditioning market access on technology transfer, and to refrain from directing overseas investment with the aim of acquiring technology to fulfil industrial policy goals. Furthermore, China agreed to make their administration and licencing requirements and processes transparent, and to protect confidentiality of sensitive technical information disclosed by foreigners during administrative, regulatory, or other review processes.[24]

---

[23] US Trade Representative, *Economic and Trade Agreement between the Government of the United States of America and the Government of the People's Republic of China*. See also Virgil Bisio, Charles Horne, Ann Listerud, Kaj Malden, Leyton Nelson, Nargiza Salidjanova, and Suzanna Stephens, "The US-China 'Phase One' Deal: A Backgrounder".

[24] US Trade Representative, *Economic and Trade Agreement between the Government of the United States of America and the Government of the People's Republic of China*. See also: Virgil Bisio, Charles Horne, Ann Listerud, Kaj Malden, Leyton Nelson, Nargiza Salidjanova, and Suzanna Stephens, "The US-China 'Phase One' Deal: A Backgrounder".

Another area of contention in the US–China trade conflict addressed in the Phase One deal is that of exchange rate practices. In chapter 5, China and the US confirmed that they are bound by the IMF Articles of Agreement to avoid manipulating exchange rates to gain an unfair competitive advantage, and both parties agreed to achieve and maintain a market-determined exchange rate regime and refrain from competitive devaluations or targeting exchange rates for competitive purposes, including through large scale interventions in currency markets.[25]

3)   Financial Services

A further area covered by the Phase One agreement is financial services. Here, the two countries made commitments on issues related to banking services, credit rating services, electronic payment services, financial asset management services, insurance services, and securities, fund management, and future services. In this context, both countries made several commitments to promote fair, effective, and non-discriminatory access for each other's financial services and service providers. For example, China agreed to allow US owned credit rating service suppliers to: rate domestic bonds sold to international investors; accept applications from US electronic payment service suppliers to become bank card clearing institutions; allow US financial service suppliers to apply for asset management company licences; remove the foreign equity cap in life, pension, and health insurance sectors; eliminate foreign equity limits; and allow US owned service

---

[25] US Trade Representative, *Economic and Trade Agreement between the Government of the United States of America and the Government of the People's Republic of China*. See also: Virgil Bisio, Charles Horne, Ann Listerud, Kaj Malden, Leyton Nelson, Nargiza Salidjanova, and Suzanna Stephens, "The US-China 'Phase One' Deal: A Backgrounder".

suppliers to participate in the securities, fund management, and futures sectors. In addition, China agreed to remove restrictions on investment, reduce burdensome regulations, and expeditiously review pending licence applications of US companies in its domestic banking, credit rating, electronic payment, asset management, insurance, and securities industries. Similarly, the US also affirmed its commitment not to discriminate against Chinese financial service providers and agreed to expeditiously review pending requests by Chinese financial institutions.[26]

4)   Dispute Resolution

Finally, the Phase One deal concludes with a chapter on a new dispute resolution process. This section of the agreement outlines a consultative process of dispute resolution. If either the US or the Chinese government believes that the other party is not complying with terms of the deal, the party complained against would complete an assessment of the complaints and designated officials would begin consultations. The consultations would proceed to progressively higher levels of officials, from the designated officials up to the Deputy US Trade Representative and the designated Vice Minister of China, and finally to the US Trade Representative and the Vice Premier of China. If the complaint cannot be resolved through consultations, the complaining party can respond by suspending an obligation under agreement or adopting proportionate remedial measures. In addition, the deal allows either side to

---

[26]   US Trade Representative, *Economic and Trade Agreement between the Government of the United States of America and the Government of the People's Republic of China.* See also: Virgil Bisio, Charles Horne, Ann Listerud, Kaj Malden, Leyton Nelson, Nargiza Salidjanova, and Suzanna Stephens, "The US-China 'Phase One' Deal: A Backgrounder".

provide written notice of withdrawal from the agreement if it believes the other party is acting in bad faith.[27]

C)   BEYOND PHASE ONE

1)   An Incomplete Deal: What is Missing from the Phase One Agreement?

First, while the Trump Administration committed to tariff reductions on a large volume of trade, tariffs will remain in place on about $370 billion out of $550 billion in total US imports from China. On average, the Phase One deal imposes US tariffs on Chinese imports at 19 percent, a substantial increase from 3 percent in 2018. Thus, the Phase One deal is still far from a complete tariff reduction to pre-trade war levels.

Second, in terms of China's commitment to increase purchases of US products, many are sceptical that China will be able to ramp up purchases so quickly. As of August 2020, China has purchased only around half of their year-to-date targets, and one third of their overall purchase commitment for 2020.[28] In addition, some commentators are concerned that the agreement would require the Chinese government or its agencies to engage in more micro-management of the economy, with state trading companies doing most of

---

[27] US Trade Representative, *Economic and Trade Agreement between the Government of the United States of America and the Government of the People's Republic of China*. See also: Virgil Bisio, Charles Horne, Ann Listerud, Kaj Malden, Leyton Nelson, Nargiza Salidjanova, and Suzanna Stephens, "The US-China 'Phase One' Deal: A Backgrounder".

[28] Chad P. Bown, "US-China Phase One Tracker: China's Purchases of US Goods", PIIE (September 25, 2020), online: <https://www.piie.com/research/piie-charts/us-china-phase-one-tracker-chinas-purchases-us-goods>.

the buying in order to meet the ambitious targets.[29] This would further expand the Chinese state's role in economic decision-making. In addition, China may need to divert purchases away from other countries, including some US trade allies. Similarly, for the US to meet its side of the agreement, it may need to divert exports away from other countries to increase sales to China. These actions may in turn undermine the WTO's Most Favoured Nation rules that require equal treatment of trading partners.[30]

Third, many commentators have pointed out that the Phase One deal fails to address the critical issue of subsidies, which is at the heart of the China–US trade conflict. Labelled by many commentators as the "giant hole" in the deal, the issue of Chinese subsidies to its state-owned enterprises was not mentioned in the text of the agreement.[31] During the early phase of the negotiation process, President Trump insisted that he hoped to resolve all outstanding trade issues in a single, comprehensive agreement, and in the early rounds of negotiations, the two parties discussed issues related to China's industrial subsidies. However, China resisted structural changes, and subsidies reduction commitments were removed from the final Phase One deal.[32] The Trump Administration recognized

---

[29] Finbarr Bermingham, "China's Trade War Deal 'May Be Doomed from the Start' as Scepticism Mounts over Capacity to Buy US Products", *South China Morning Post* (January 21, 2020), online: <https://www.scmp.com/economy/china-economy/article/3047018/chinas-trade-war-deal-may-be-doomed-start-scepticism-mounts>.

[30] Virgil Bisio, Charles Horne, Ann Listerud, Kaj Malden, Leyton Nelson, Nargiza Salidjanova, and Suzanna Stephens, "The US-China 'Phase One' Deal: A Backgrounder".

[31] Megan Cassella, "The 'Giant Hole' in Trump's New China Deal", *Politico* (January 15, 2020), online: <https://www.politico.com/news/2020/01/15/hole-trump-china-trade-deal-099327>.

[32] David J. Lynch, "Initial US-China Trade Deal Has Major Hole: Beijing's Massive Business Subsidies", *The Washington Post* (December 31, 2019), online: <https://www.washingtonpost

that some key issues remain unresolved and would be left for future negotiations, and potentially a "phase two" agreement.[33] However, to date, there have been no firm plans for such negotiations.

Fourth, while the Phase One agreement addressed a number of important issues such as intellectual property and technology transfer, the solution offered by the agreement is incomplete and many uncertainties remain. On the contentious issue of intellectual property protection, many commentators are concerned about the vagueness and enforceability of China's commitments. For example, the agreement did not propose judicial reforms in China's new national appellate IP court, new internet courts, and local specialized IP courts at the intermediate level. The agreement also contains no obligations on China's side to publish more trade secret cases and to make court dockets more available to the public.[34] While the agreement requires Chinese courts to issue injunctions for urgent cases of potential trade secret disclosure, Chinese judges can be induced not to find cases "urgent" due to the lack of an independent judiciary.[35]

Finally, an important issue not addressed by the Phase One agreement is the conflict between the US and China over emerging technologies such as Artificial Intelligence (AI)

.com/business/economy/initial-us-china-trade-deal-has-major-hole-beijings-massive-business-subsidies/2019/12/30/>.

[33]   Chad P. Bown, "Unappreciated Hazards of the US-China Phase One Deal", *Peterson Institute for International Economics* (January 21, 2020), online: <https://www.piie.com/blogs/trade-and-investment-policy-watch/unappreciated-hazards-us-china-phase-one-deal>.

[34]   Mark Cohen, "The Phase 1 IP Agreement: Its Fans and Discontents", *China IPR* (January 21, 2020), online: <https://www.law.berkeley.edu/wp-content/uploads/2020/05/CohenMark1.pdf>.

[35]   Virgil Bisio, Charles Horne, Ann Listerud, Kaj Malden, Leyton Nelson, Nargiza Salidjanova, and Suzanna Stephens, "The US-China 'Phase One' Deal: A Backgrounder".

and the 5G network. The Trump Administration espoused a technology policy that rests on restricting the flow of technology to China and investing more in emerging technologies domestically to promote US innovation. For example, the US government has cut its supply of core technologies to Chinese tech companies, proposed a 30 percent increase in spending on AI and quantum and information sciences, banned the Chinese company Huawei from buying American semiconductors which are critical components of its 5G technology, and issued orders that would ban Chinese social media apps such as TikTok and Wechat from operating in the US if they are not sold by their Chinese parent companies. More recently, the Trump Administration's restrictions on exports of high-tech products to China cut off one of the few sources of hope for China to reach the volume of imports targeted in the Phase One deal. High-tech products such as American semiconductors and chipmaking equipment was one of the most robust areas of American exports to China, yet the new export control regime led to sharp drops in their sales. These restrictions are mainly driven by concerns regarding Huawei and the potential threat that it poses to national security through its supply of 5G infrastructure like base stations. Specifically, the US is concerned that China's laws could compel Huawei to collect and turn over personal, government, or military information to the Chinese government.[36]

In response, China has devised a counterstrategy that rests on the rapid development of core technologies to reduce its dependence on the US. For example, recently, China's National People's Congress launched a five-year plan with nearly $1.4 trillion in investments for building "new infra-

---

[36] Chad P. Bown, "How Trump's Export Curbs on Semiconductors and Equipment Hurt the US Technology Sector," *PIIE* (September 28, 2020), online: <https://www.piie.com/blogs/trade-and-investment-policy-watch/how-trumps-export-curbs-semiconductors-and-equipment-hurt-us>.

structure" through emerging technologies such as AI, 5G, the Industrial Internet, and others. In particular, China hopes to reduce its dependence on American semiconductors, and to this end has established a $29 billion semiconductor fund and other policies to support chip industries. As Adam Segal argues,[37] these actions have set the contours of a "tech cold war" where leaders of both China and the US are aiming to fast track domestic technological advancement by making it a matter of national security. A Deutsche Bank report estimates that the tech war will cost more than $3.5 trillion over the next five years. Yet despite the seriousness of this conflict between China and the US over technological pre-eminence in emerging technology sectors, this critical issue was not addressed in the Phase One deal between the two countries.

2)   Fundamental Flaws of the Phase One Deal

On a more fundamental level, critics of the agreement argue that the Phase One deal represents a misunderstanding of global trade and undermines the interests of the international community. For example, Yukon Huang and Jeremy Smith argue that the framework of the trade deal is conceptually flawed and will likely result in damage to the rules-based international trade regime. First, the ambitious target for China to increase purchases of US goods and services by 92 percent above 2017 levels will rely on state-managed purchases which violates globally accepted practices. Second, the countries' bilateral trade commitments ignore the more fundamental fact that trade relies on multilateral relationships. As such, achieving the targets requires trade to be diverted from other partners, and this diversion would contravene

---

[37]   Adam Segal, "The Coming Tech Cold War with China", *Foreign Affairs* (September 9, 2020), online: <https://www .foreignaffairs.com/articles/north-america/2020-09-09/coming-tech -cold-war-china>.

WTO disciplines and is likely to drag affected parties into complex disputes. Finally, the dispute resolution framework in the agreement compromises multilateralism. Given the near inevitability of a violation, the dispute resolution framework is a central part of the agreement. Under this framework, decisions are quickly elevated to the US Trade Representative and China's Vice Premier, and if they cannot agree on a solution, the government of the US or China would be able to adopt remedial measures such as tariffs. If the opposing side determines that these remedial measures are in bad faith, the only recourse available would be to withdraw from the agreement. Thus, Huang and Smith argue that this deal is a complete rejection of an international adjudicative process, reinforces efforts to weaken the WTO, and promotes bilateralism and managed trade rather than multilateralism.[38]

---

[38] Yukon Huang and Jeremy Smith, "Trump's Phase One Deal with China Misunderstands Global Trade", *Carnegie Endowment for International Peace* (January 28, 2020), online: <https://carnegieendowment.org/2020/01/28/trump-s-phase-one-deal-with-china-misunderstands-global-trade-pub-80919>.

VIII. Conclusion: the future of international trading

At the present juncture in international economic relations, there is no shortage of doomsayers. Even one of the most respected academic journals in the field, the *Journal of International Economic Law*, recently published a special issue entitled "The Era of Disintegration". While there is no gainsaying the serious contemporary sources of turbulence and perturbation in international economic relations, I believe that these doomsday scenarios are exaggerated or at least premature. As I pointed out in my brief historical review of international trade at the outset of this book, people have been trading with each other since the beginning of recorded history, across the boundaries of clans, tribes, villages, cities, and countries. While early and very basic trading relations were often able to be sustained through rudimentary customs and norms that emerged from repeat dealings, as trading relations expanded over time, space, and range of parties, it became increasingly recognized that the stability and security of these relations required a more formal legal infrastructure. It seems implausible that contemporary sources of international economic turbulence are likely to refute or reverse this basic historical imperative.

Moreover, many of the more extreme doomsday or cataclysmic scenarios for the future of the international economic system are premised on a Golden Age of international economic integration that has rarely, if ever, existed. While, as I pointed out early in this book, the founders of the GATT in 1947 subscribed to the view that a common set of ground rules governing trading relations among all countries was an ideal that was likely first to give full play to concepts of comparative advantage and second to reduce geopolitical tensions that had led to two catastrophic world wars in the first half of the 20th century, this was never more than an aspiration, and indeed an aspiration that was increasingly challenged in its own terms. First, only 23 countries were initially parties to the GATT, and they were predominantly western oriented developed countries. Over the intervening decades, particularly during the period of decolonization beginning in the 1950s, the GATT membership expanded to its current membership of 164 countries, many of which joined in quite recent years – most Arab oil exporting countries, China, and Russia only in the past two decades. While many developing countries joined the GATT from the 1950s onwards, in a striking irony many repudiated two central pillars of the original GATT – nondiscrimination and reciprocity – by claiming special and differential treatment permitting them to discriminate against imports in order to promote infant industries or for balance of payments reasons, and by claiming nonreciprocal preferences from developed countries with respect to access to their markets. Both of these claims were recognized by amendments to the GATT in the mid-1950s and mid-1960s. In effect, many developing countries elected to become largely non-participants in ongoing GATT negotiations. Moreover, the Cold War that broke out between the Soviet Union, the US, and Western Europe almost immediately after the formation of the GATT led to the formation in turn of rival trading blocs – in the case of the Soviet Union, Comecon, and in the case of Western Europe, the emergence of the European Union. Even amongst western developed countries, while successive rounds of GATT negotiation dramatically reduced overall tariff levels on average, many tariff peaks remained, sometimes running into several hundred percent, especially in the agricultural sector, yielding quite a variable geometry in terms of tariff patterns by country and product category.

It is important in this context to note the shifting strands of thinking on economic development policy over the post-war period and the role of international trade policy in broader theories of economic development.[1] In the early post-war period extending into the heyday of decolonization, development theorists in both developed and developing countries widely subscribed to state-led, big push theories of development predicated on pervasive market failures in the economies of developing countries. These theories in turn provided the intellectual predicate for special and differential status for developing countries in the GATT. In the light of mixed to disappointing experience with many of these policies, beginning in the mid-1970s and through the 1980s development thinking was largely stood on its head by the adoption in many development circles of the so-called Washington Consensus which called for a larger role for private markets and a smaller role for the state in developing countries through policies of privatization, deregulation, and international trade and investment liberalization.

The intellectual premises of these policies provided an important impetus for the Uruguay Round of multilateral trade negotiations from 1986 to 1993, where an extremely expansive negotiating agenda extending well beyond border measures such as tariffs and quotas to services, intellectual property, subsidies, foreign investment, product standards, and government procurement was framed on an all or nothing, single undertaking basis, with relatively minor dispensations or exceptions for developing countries typically taking the form of extended transition periods for implementation. While some gains were realized by developing countries in terms of modest agricultural liberalization commitments by developed countries and the phasing out of the Multi-Fibre Arrangement,

---

[1]   Michael Trebilcock, "Between Theories of Trade and Development and the Future of the World Trading System" (2015) 16 *Journal of World Investment and Trade* 122.

concomitant commitments by developing countries with respect to intellectual property rights, product standards, subsidies, and services may have outweighed the benefits of the so-called "Grand Bargain" – the apogee of the aspiration of a common set of ground rules for all trading nations.

As the Uruguay Round was being concluded in 1993, the sands of thinking on economic development were shifting once again. Reflecting an increasing modesty on the part of economists and development agencies as to any common set of prescriptions for sustainable long-term economic growth, both development thinking and development policies on the ground increasingly came to recognize that appropriate prescriptions for economic development policies were highly context specific and very much a function of particular countries' histories, culture, geography, politics, ethnic and religious makeup, and so on, leading often to strong forms of particularized path dependency.[2]

These shifting sands in development thinking became evident immediately after the close of the Uruguay Round. First, the devastating impact of the HIV/AIDS epidemic for many developing countries, especially in Africa, led to intense critiques of the Trade-Related Intellectual Property Rights Agreement reached during the Uruguay Round as severely restricting access by poor citizens of developing countries to essential medicines, typically held under patent by western pharmaceutical companies. Similar critiques were levied

---

[2]   Dani Rodrik, *One Economics Many Recipes: Globalization, Institutions and Economic Growth* (Princeton University Press, 2008); Charles Kenny, *Getting Better: Why Global Development Is Succeeding – and How We Can Improve the World Even More*; Abhijit V. Banerjee and Esther Duflo, *Good Economics for Hard Times: Better Answers to Our Biggest Problems*; Matt Andrews, Lant Pritchett, and Michael Woolcock, *Building State Capability: Evidence, Analysis, Action* (Oxford University Press, 2017); Michael Trebilcock and Mariana Prado, *Advanced Introduction to Law and Development* (Edward Elgar Publishing, 2nd ed., 2021).

against the Sanitary and Phytosanitary Standards Agreement and the Technical Barriers to Trade Agreement as imposing one-size-fits-all international standards on all member countries despite many differences in local conditions, preferences and capacities.

Not coincidentally, the close of the Uruguay Round was the beginning of the proliferation of Preferential Trade Agreements (PTAs), sometimes between developed countries, more often between developed and developing countries, and increasingly frequently between or among developing countries themselves. The North American Free Trade Agreement came into force at the beginning of 1994. Over the next decade or so the EU dramatically expanded its membership to include former Eastern bloc countries; a new regional trading bloc emerged amongst 20 Caribbean counties and dependences (Caricom); Mercosur was entered into by four Latin American countries; various regional trading blocs emerged in Africa, culminating recently in a pan-African free trade agreement amongst about 50 countries; Canada has recently entered into a free trade agreement with the EU (CETA); the Trans-Pacific Partnership Agreement was negotiated amongst 12 Asian and South Pacific counties (with the US Trump Administration subsequently withdrawing); the previous US administration had initiated discussions with the EU over a Transatlantic Trade and Investment Partnership (from which the Trump Administration also withdrew); and 16 Asian countries have recently negotiated a Comprehensive Regional Economic Partnership, including China (from which India subsequently withdrew), and with significant overlapping membership with the TPPA. The EU has recently signed a free trade agreement with Japan and is pursuing negotiations of free trade agreements with Mexico, Australia, and New Zealand. A new US administration may revive membership in the TPPA and negotiations with the EU over a TTIP.

In the meantime, after a false start in Seattle in late 1999, a new round of multilateral trade negotiations under the auspices of the WTO was launched in Doha in 2001, but has recently petered out after almost two decades of largely fruitless negotiations, with the exception of the Trade Facilitation Agreement designed to streamline customs administration in member countries. While the round was officially designated the "development round" at the outset in an attempt to assuage the concerns of developing countries over what many considered an unbalanced "Grand Bargain" struck during the Uruguay Round, and despite efforts to appease some of their concerns over negotiating overreach by removing issues such as competition policy, foreign investment, and labour rights from the negotiating agenda, consensus on remaining issues among developing and developed countries has proved unattainable. Exacerbating paralysis of the political organs of the WTO governed by the consensus principle, the quasi-judicial dispute resolution regime has become seriously dysfunctional as a result of the US Trump Administration's refusal to agree to the appointment of new Appellate Body members (which may change with a new Administration).

As one reflects on the changing currents of thinking on the relationship between international trade and economic development and the changing configuration of legal regimes governing trading relationships, one thing is clear: there is no shortage of international trade and investment law emanating from an ever proliferating range of sources. Clearly, the underlying vision or dream of the founders of the GATT in 1947 of a common set of ground rules governing all international trading relations has largely proven a pipe dream. However, conversely, the world does not seem to be about to descend into extreme forms of autarchy, let alone anarchy. To recall and adapt a quip from Mark Twain, "the rumours of my demise are greatly exaggerated".

While, as I have noted earlier in this book, I am sceptical of grand predictions about the future, it seems increasingly likely that international trading relations will be dominated by various mega-regional trading blocs. However, few, if any, of these blocs will be anywhere close to self-sustaining, leaving open the challenge of structuring relations between these blocs. In this respect, the multilateral system as exemplified by the WTO may in the future serve an invaluable function in providing a forum for inter-bloc negotiations, much as the EU does now in negotiating trade policies on behalf of all its member states and enabling member countries of these blocs, especially poorer developing countries, to pool their negotiating resources and bargaining leverage beyond what they have been able to achieve to date in informal coalition bargaining within the WTO. To facilitate such bargaining, I have previously proposed the abandonment of the paralyzing consensus principle in favour of facilitating plurilateral agreements within the WTO that are open to subsequent accession by the other WTO members on a conditional Most Favoured Nation basis, that is, accepting similar obligations to existing signatories in return for similar entitlements.[3] At present, the WTO Agreement (Art. X (9)) requires consensus of all members to incorporate a plurilateral agreement within the WTO which compounds the paralysis engendered by the general consensus principle by conferring veto rights on countries that are not parties to such an agreement. Amending this provision in the WTO Agreement seems much more promising than moving to a majority voting regime within the WTO, which larger trading powers would strenuously resist in the face of the prospect of being routinely out-voted by a majority of small, mostly developing countries, or moving to a trade weighted majority voting regime, which would provoke countervailing resistance by smaller developed and developing countries faced with the prospect of routinely being subjected to trade disciplines dictated by the major trading powers.

---

[3]   Trebilcock, "Between Theories of Trade and Development and the Future of the World Trading System".

Plurilateral agreements already have a well-established status in the multilateral system –most of the Tokyo Round Non-Tariff Barrier Codes were plurilateral, as is the current Government Procurement Agreement. Plurilateral agreements are likely to dominate the international trade law landscape in the foreseeable future. The central questions are whether they should be encouraged to find a place within the WTO or outside its framework, and whether they should be closed or open to new members prepared to pay a price of admission comparable to that of existing members. While this would entail the abandonment of the aspiration of a common set of ground rules for all trading countries, this ideal has never been fully realized in practice, and, as argued earlier in this book, denies the painful truth that economists have no strongly developed consensus on policy prescriptions for sustainable long-term economic growth and the appropriate role of trade policies in such prescriptions.

Within this institutional architecture, the most prominent contemporary friction points that require resolution have been canvassed in the body of this book, along with various proposals for mitigating these frictions. Amongst the most acute at present are those relating to: a) subsidies that distort comparative advantage in international trade and appear to have no independent, non-trade related justifications; b) the extent of the protection of intellectual property rights in international trade agreements, including access to essential medicines; c) the scope of national security exceptions in trade and investment agreements, particularly as they pertain to trade and investment in emerging high-technology sectors; d) the scope for deviations from trade and investment disciplines to address pressing environmental problems, in particular measures designed to induce serious international convergence on effective policies for addressing the grave risks of climate change.

I have no easy panaceas for the resolution of these critical friction points, but they seem no more daunting than the challenges facing the founders of the GATT and the other Bretton Woods institutions in building a new international economic architecture in the ashes of World War II and an earlier World War, pandemic, and Great Depression in the first half of the 20th century. It would seem a tragedy that we need to re-learn the lessons that the architects of the Bretton Woods agreement, the United Nations and its many agencies, and other agencies of global governance bequeathed to us based on their bitter experience of the first half of the 20th century. We should aspire to do better than to condemn ourselves to forgetting the lessons of history.

Index